GUITARS & CIGARS AND TIKI BARS

ONE GUY'S GUIDE TO SPIRITUALITY

JOHN J. MATHIS

Guitars, Cigars and Tiki Bars

Guitars, Cigars and Tiki Bars

Copyright © 2019
John J Mathis
All rights reserved.
ISBN: 987-1-68-966191-1

Guitars, Cigars and Tiki Bars

CONTENTS

Forward	i
Chapter 1	Pg 1
Chapter 2	Pg 15
Chapter 3	Pg 30
Chapter 4	Pg 50
Chapter 5	Pg 73
Chapter 6	Pg 88
Chapter 7	Pg 108
Chapter 8	Pg 125
Chapter 9	Pg 136
Chapter 10	Pg 152
Chapter 12	Pg 171
Chapter 13	Pg 198
Chapter 14	Pg 219
Epilogue	Pg 230

FORWARD

OK, I lied.

When I wrote my first book, I said it would probably be my last, knowing all along that this was the conceit of a writer. Why? Because a writer writes; it is an obsession that cannot be held in check. It is also true that a writer is one who rewrites the rewrite they have previously rewritten (Shameless plug in four…three…two…).

When I self-published *The Alchemist's Heir* – a story of a high-school student who gets some metaphysical schooling from his grandfather to help him deal with bullies—it was my attempt to balance "The Equation." I have a lifelong compulsion to offset something bad with something good. When my mom passed away, something craptastic had happened, so I wanted to put something wonderful out into the world. Based on the responses I received, I thought I'd had another go at it. Ergo, a writer writes—again. OK, still.

That book of "fiction" was a catharsis because I had been bullied: by bullies, by crap jobs, and by crappier life circumstances. And really, who hasn't been bullied? At some point, we have all been in its path when that tornado of life has raged across the sewage containment pond and headed in our direction.

But what if I told you I was thankful for the brown rain? In it, I saw reality and I was grateful. I saw them as stabilizing elements in my very unusual life. These anchors kept me grounded amidst the extraordinary metaphysical whirlwind I was discovering—or re-discovering depending on your philosophy regarding the chicken-versus-the-egg debate.

For some, turning life challenges into potential growth opportunities is called faith. Others may call it inertia. I'm the storyteller here, so I'm calling it Obstinate Spirituality (OS). My

OS is comprised of astral projection off-planet; remote viewing peculiarities on or in the Earth; charging up people, places, and things with Reiki; and interacting with non-corporeal entities. Put that in your bong and smoke it.

Put that in your bong and smoke it.

When you spend your nightly slumber off-planet, exploring the dark side of the moon and chatting up the beings posted there, a fender-bender or a kidney stone from time to time helps keep things in perspective.

Never have I told my entire story. At first, I was afraid of familial rejection. Then, I was afraid of jeopardizing my employment. However, my discoveries are so amazing that I was bursting to share at least some of them with someone. For more than a decade, a variety of people—select friends, passing acquaintances, even complete strangers—have urged me to tell my whole story. Not just the near-death experience (NDE); not just the remote viewing; not just the Reiki; not just the ghost hunting—and finding—but the whole enchilada with the unifying rationale being that others would find it beneficial.

I wish I could say I have found the courage to let my freak flag fly, but the truth is that I have hit a point of super- saturation. It is time for me to come out of the metaphysical closet.

Frankly, it is one of the scariest things I have ever done.

There will be haters, trolls, fundamentalists, and skeptics. To you I say, before you call "BS" on me, please consider this: I recognize that I chose an extraordinarily unusual series of coping mechanisms. I believe selective dissociation is a way many others have also chosen to cope and have likewise elected to hide. My selection was ...unique.

Many people have healthy coping strategies for dealing with unpleasant situations: daydreaming, journaling, jogging, or coloring. Some have rather poor coping skills for which the tobacco, alcohol, firearms, and narcotics industries are thankful. So are Weight Watchers®, Jack Daniels®, and Trojan™ (ribbed for their marketing pleasure). Right or wrong, the aforementioned strategies are unified in the sense that they are socially acceptable. Hey everyone, I'm gonna go kill this bottle of Jack and then chat with the ancestors. Ri-i-ight.

Maybe I should have gone with desensitization theory? Maybe this is why I keep dreaming of Archangels lounging on my couch and drinking my beer? More on that later.

Maybe this is why I keep dreaming of Archangels lounging on my couch and drinking my beer.

As a child of abuse, my escape was hiding in a drainage culvert, writing my own poetry, and entering into a state of consciousness, which some will call "classic dissociative," and others will call "out of body." A couple years later, I found the book *Far Journeys* by Robert Monroe. It not only legitimized my internal escapism, but it also acted as a textbook giving me direction and instruction when I needed it most. It blurred the line between science fiction—which I enjoyed—and fringe science.

I began seeking out similar strange books and stories as they were gateways into another person's imagination. When I was looking to escape an unpleasant situation, it was an amazing place to hide. Truly, you are temporarily rejecting your reality and borrowing another belonging to someone else. It is one of the reasons why reading someone's diary is such a temptation. It's also why I started wearing copious amounts of Polo cologne in high school.

I soon had filled my adolescent head with arcane books and ideas surrounding ghosts, self-hypnosis, and spiritual practices of indigenous peoples. Later, I would discover the Silva Method which helped me categorize the discoveries I had made, and assisted me as I developed my own operating system—another OS.

I have been told a metaphysical practice is nothing more than a self-reinforcing delusion. It very well may be. Other times I have heard it called "pseudoscience." My response: So what? I am no more delusional than those who believe in an imaginary deity who is really bad with cash flow, holy wood scraps, or sacred undergarments. Whatever you want to call it, my OS has kept me moving in this world when nothing else could have.

At its core, my OS encourages me to be good and to do good...absent the guilt and negativity associated with organized religion. Since I am not committed to the dogma of any one religion, I am not constrained by them either. I don't play for any one team, and in doing so, some will say I am cheating. I'm OK with that.

My OS has facilitated some amazing experiences that blow the doors off any church service, video game, movie, outdoor adventure, recreational sex, or drug use I have ever known—so far.

A bold statement from a Scorpio.

For example, because of my NDE, I know I am forever loved by God, regardless of the aforementioned debauchery. Because of my astral projection, I know we are unique *and* not alone in the solar system. Because of my nursing and Reiki training, I have been able to ease at least some suffering for those who struggle to see the rainbow during their own brown rainstorms.

I have even been able to communicate with several of my former selves in past lifetimes—prior to each of their

physical deaths—to calm that individual Self, administer Reiki, and ease that Self through its transition.

Some call this process "soul fragment retrieval"; some say it's an acid trip. You decide.

Ironically, none of this is new! My experiences are not unique to me. You can find these ideas among the writings of Vedic masters, indigenous healers, Emanuel Swedenborg, Nicola Tesla, Jose Silva, Robert Monroe, and Raymond Moody. All I did was put them in my mental martini mixer and asked to be both shaken and stirred from an ordinary life. Mission accomplished.

Are you still with me? Sweet! If you haven't burned this book, run to church to wash your eyes with holy water, or turned into a pillar of salt, then I say, "Good!" because we're going to have a great ride! Like a good groin muscle massage, everyone needs their reality stretched now and again.

Like a good groin muscle massage, everyone needs their reality stretched now and again.

Being a former welfare kid, driving around nice neighborhoods was our vacation. It was interesting to see what other people called home, to see how others lived, and to broaden my mental construct of what life had to offer. Perhaps you did this, too. Now, imagine doing the very same thing with your consciousness. What neighborhoods would you explore if time, distance, and terra firma were no longer impediments to your curiosity?

Having come this far with me, take one more step and meet the "voice" of the book itself.

Many of us have become passive eavesdroppers due to the societal phenomena that surrounds us with mobile phone-equipped people who, in turn, spend their agile workdays encompassed by cubicle walls only five feet high.

In reading this book, you will be listening to one side of a conversation. Why? I see this as the backdrop for the stage upon which we all currently play. I also like the idea of allowing you, the reader, to provide the other side of the conversation. Since the interjected voice is yours, it will be more familiar. As such, the reading experience itself will be more engaging.

Then again, I could be completely wrong. That's what makes it exciting! It could be the creation of a new style of literature ... or it could be gone like a fart in a hurricane.

I'm not sure if this work will help you out of any particular metaphysical malaise that you may be experiencing. Nevertheless, it will be a distraction from your personal comic opera. At the very least, hope you will find it entertaining. But I also hope to give you new ideas to ponder. Ultimately, that's why you buy a book, right?

Oh, and BTW... I'm not lying.

CHAPTER 1

"Humor is tragedy plus time." – Mark Twain.

Stop me if you've heard this one...

Mr. Bear and Mr. Rabbit are both taking a shit in the woods under the same tree. Breaking with male bathroom protocol, Mr. Bear not only makes eye contact but also attempts some small talk. He asks Mr. Rabbit if he has any problems with shit sticking to his fur.

Recognizing that Mr. Bear has broken with men's room etiquette, but also not wanting to offend the towering omnivore—who is quite obviously making room for more food—Mr. Rabbit responds. No, he has 99 problems, but shitty fur isn't one of them.

So, the bear wipes his ass with the rabbit.

Boom!

I don't care if you are 15 or 115 years old, that joke is funny.

I tell you, some days you are the rabbit and some days you are the bear.

Oh. So you've never wiped your ass with someone?

I respectfully disagree. We've all done it.

Hmm...OK, have you ever taken someone's food out of the fridge at work? Have you ever cut someone off in traffic? Have you ever made someone go around you while driving in the fast lane? Have you ever shown up at a retail establishment a few minutes before closing? Well then, abracadabra! You've wiped your ass with someone else.

It doesn't matter if it was intentional or not. You need not be aware of your douchebaggery in order to be a douche bag. It is just one of the rules in the Game of Life, Human Edition.

Those aren't my rules, bro.

No, they are not my rules, but I know the guy who made them.

Yes, seriously.

The Big Kahuna.

The Big Kahuna, the Big Cheese, the first Original Gangster, the first ODB.

You're gonna make me say it? Fine. It's God.

Yes, God-God.

Don't look at me in that tone of voice, brother. I speak the truth.

How do I know? Dude, I nearly died from multiple organ system failure. While in a coma, I had an Near Death Experience and I got to talk to God.

Yes, seriously.

No, I am not joking.

I met God. We chatted. I got a tour of the Universe. I met deceased relatives. I saw all these geometric figures. I was introduced to the heavenly choirs and got to gig with them.

Yes, really…and it gets better!

I was shown the real illusions of time, distance, and separation. I saw the energetic connection among all things in the Universe, past, present, and future! I received my own "commandments" to use for the rest of my life. I was given a list of messages to share with the people of Earth when I returned. Through it all, I was a part of unconditional love…that rapturous bliss…that eternal contentment and satisfaction that is being one with The Creator!

No, I wasn't on acid, you dumb ass.

It wasn't 'shrooms, either.

No. The fact is that I had just been removed from life support.

Yes, I think it is real.

No, I am not shitting you.

No, I am not lying. I am not jerking your chain.

Dude, it's responses like this that have taught me to just shut my mouth and keep everything to myself.

Why?

Because, brother, this message is sacred! It is important. It is timely. But the more time I spend back on Earth, the more I think this planet needs an enema and not my damn message.

Well, honestly, I thought it needed an enema before the near-death thingy.

Guitars, Cigars and Tiki Bars

Look, man. I have been questioning why I am playing this game of life since day one when I landed in an incubator. I questioned it even more when my best friend died; I was 9 years old. I have had nothing but questions ever since. Don Henley was right when he sang, "The more I know, the less I understand. All the things I thought I knew, I'm learning again."

Yeah, the Eagles...the trump card of the Dad Rock genre.

Yes, that is a deep rabbit hole. I'm here to tell you that rabbit holes are infinite in both depth and number. Some people get lost in a single rabbit hole because of its gravitas...or because of its seductive nature.

What's the real seduction? The real seduction is learning there is more than one rabbit hole. Then, to know that you can combine the power of them into one marvelous adventure.

Oh, so now you are curious about my God story? Well, I won't tell you.

Yes, really.

Why?

First, I think it will be the equivalent of skywriting on a cloudy night. Second, it is a subjective experience. Until you know the subject, which is me, you will fail to comprehend the magnitude of it.

The real irony here is that I *want* to tell you my story.

I want to tell you my story because I think it is like no other. It is sacred to me. And someday, somehow, I hope to meet somebody who says, "Me too." But the pendulum has swung the other way. I returned wanting to assist my fellow man in any way that I could. Now, if you cut me off in traffic, I'll tell you to sneeze so you can pop your head out of your ass.

Dude, I have been shut down so many times before! Why fall on your sword when people will just complain about the cost of having the carpet cleaned?

Really?

Wow! Well, yes…I accept your apology. You are a better man than I thought.

Seriously. An apology is both an act of contrition and evidence of internal fortitude. Thank you. You are one of a very few.

Sure, I'll have a drink with you. How about a Glenfiddich? Splash of water to open it up and one ice cube.

Thanks!

So, I was saying? Oh, yes…I have been told by many that my story would be helpful to others. But I only tell fragments. Having been a teacher and a nurse, I can honestly say I like helping others. It's in my DNA. It is my operating system. It's in my OS… in more connotations than one. But my sharing more than a fragment of my story can be overwhelming.

Dude, I've made ministers weep and therapists run out of ink. I've made people get up and leave during outpatient therapy because it overwhelmed them.

How would it start? My story would start out weird because it isn't about God. It's about the things you bring home with you.

No, I didn't bring home a barfly or a dumpster find…on this occasion. It starts with some stinky, dog-eared books from a garage sale that I brought home. A crazy box of books for three bucks.

Seriously, who would think three beat up paperback books would change not just the trajectory of my life, but my perception of life on this ball of mud we call home?

I told you it was weird, bro.

Look, I agree it is not a story that is commonplace. I have had some people roll their eyes or flat out say I am lying. Totally reasonable. People work hard at creating their reality, and dropping contrary knowledge is like dropping a deuce in a prom punch bowl.

I can't do or say enough to change a person. Change is part of everyone's own Internal Affairs office. But for those who have shared in some of my experiences, just knowing there is another person out there who has experienced some of the same things is cathartic.

Cathartic, not Catholic. Jesus, does drinking affect your herring?

Well, at least you caught that one! See what I did there? Caught...herring.

Are you sure you want to hear this?

If you want the story, I'm willing to try it one more time. Who knows? Maybe this time is the right time. Even if the haters hadn't existed along the way, perhaps I needed some time for the story to come together. Like a good batch of hooch, it needed time to ferment.

Brother, you bought me a drink and offered up an apology. Let me politely offer you an escape from some old fartknocker sitting in a faux Tiki bar, with a fading sunset both inside and out, and prattling on about my life and mystery school machinations.

All right, let the dissuasion begin!

First, it's a crap story containing child abuse, divorce, self-sabotage, bankruptcy, deaths and abandonment. Not exactly Hallmark or Kodak moments. It's where fortitude meets 'suck-titude'.

Awesome intro, right?

OK, going on.

Specifically, it has some smaller stories, which are equally crappy, about the responsibility of turning off life support on a parent...how one marches onward through the suicide of the other parent...and the hundred other little deaths that follow.

Yes—holy shit.

I tried telling my story once to a minister. With teary eyes, she replied, "I have no idea what to do with you." Like I said, run away now.

Look, these milestone events are certainly skid marks on the tighty-whities highway of life. But they are not unique to the human condition. The fact that all these events happened to one person is unusual, but not unheard of. Truth be told, it was the normalcy of these tragedies that grounded me.

Yes, normalcy.

What I mean by that is these tragedies were grounding for me; they are all part of the normal human experience. They helped me come to terms with the abnormal—the exceptional—human experiences that were also a big part of my life.

What do I mean by exceptional human experiences? Excellent question! Since you hit the hook, I'll let you taste the bait.

One of my exceptional human experiences, or EHEs if you will, is my process of projecting my astral body back to a former lifetime. It is from this perspective that I assist my former corporeal self through the death process. This way, I can reintegrate my soul into a more complete individual in this current lifetime.

Ha! You look like you just sat on your balls.

Too much? OK, I'll ratchet it back. I wouldn't want you to blow a head gasket.

Well, how about ghosts? You OK with that topic?

What kind? All of them. From the familiars that sat at the end of my bed for a chat to the mean ones that punched, scratched, and pursued me in my car. All that would be defined as an EHE for the one who experiences it for the first time. I just don't think it's necessarily "exceptional" anymore.

Why?

Well, my wide-eyed friend, thanks to hundreds of cable channels, ghost stories are as commonplace as a person checking their phone at a stoplight.

You laugh, but you know what I miss? I miss the old days when people picked their noses at stoplights. Some people were so enthusiastic that the word "fisting" sometimes comes to mind.

Jesus!

No worries. Spitting your drink is the same as applause when one tells a joke in a bar.

What else?

I feel my stories of remote viewing and astral projection are a bit more exceptional. It's a great way to travel. You don't need to wear anything. You don't have to check your luggage. There are almost no travel restrictions, and travel "blackout dates" have a different connotation.

Yes, that is also part of my exceptional human experience or EHE.

Well, I've found that these stories are interesting to most people, but they are not exceptional. Even remote viewing has left the world of fringe science. Now that the movie *Men Who Stare at Goats* is out there, and Project Stargate has been declassified, these Jedi warriors of the mind are now out of their proverbial closets—selling books, teaching classes, and integrating remote viewing into corporate espionage strategies.

Dude, it's Six Sigma meets *The Sixth Sense*.

No, I'm not shitting you. The mystery and adventure of projecting your consciousness into a realm where time and distance have no meaning has been co-opted by corporate America. Nothing exceptional about that. Sometimes I think the phrase should be called "industrial-military complex," instead of the other way around.

What else? Well, for a couple of years, I drew some blank stares from people when I spoke about Reiki. But its benefits, which people began to realize in the aftermath of the financial bubble-pop around 2008, contributed to a rise in the exploration of various avenues of healing called of complementary / alternative medicine.

From this crisis also arose the discovery that herbs, weeds, aromas, and such could provide some benefit. This "discovery" was common knowledge among our forebears and some indigenous peoples for thousands of years, so "re-discovery" might be a more appropriate term.

When I worked as a cancer nurse, I was pleased to see that massage was actively used when there was lymph node involvement. This catalyzed my thought that Reiki would be a welcomed adjunct therapy.

My former nurse manager thought I was crazy to suggest Reiki on the cancer floor. It was too fringe for her even though I could demonstrate its improvement of the patient experience subjectively, and objectively show that the use of nausea and pain meds would decrease.

Fortunately, Reiki is no longer a "woo-woo" word. Top cancer centers all over the world utilize Reiki as a healing modality. Hell, even Medicare guidelines have recategorized it to "under consideration." Once they figure a way to bill for it, it will be used.

Seriously, in order for me to get a blank stare from people now, I have to mention my blending of Reiki and astral projection to visit previous lifetimes. See what I did there? Three rabbit holes in one sentence! Boo-ya!

Good recovery...no ball-sitting face.

Yes, acknowledgment of past lives is another EHE. It is uncommon, but it is part of the human experience and has been acknowledged for thousands of years.

I'd say my exploration of past life regression, or PLR, has been both therapeutic and fun. I have uncovered 14 lifetimes so far and, frankly, I don't plan to spend another minute looking for more.

Because I have learned it is *this* life that matters.

Imagine your physical body as a car. You can't drive a car looking only in the rear-view mirror. You can gaze backward occasionally, but your machine is designed to propel you forward.

John Lennon referred to death as getting out of one car and into another.

If you have seen the movie, *Dead Again*, or have read any of Dr. Brian Weiss's books, I can tell you that the craziness therein is real.

Seriously, I have been black, white, yellow, red, and a few other colors. Mostly male—but female, too. When exploring past lives, the trick is remembering that you have lessons from this life to learn as well.

It's a well-constructed symphony. Your lifetimes build and build—a crescendo of experiences—like Beethoven's Ninth Symphony. With any luck, it builds to a rapturous conclusion of joy.

I think it's amazing, too. Still, there is nothing exceptional here because, thanks to Shirley MacLaine and Richard Gere, reincarnation entered the western mainstream a couple generations ago...and never left.

Good question. What was the most surprising thing I learned? One of my personal discoveries from PLR was when I learned that, rather than working on a comprehensive shopping list from the cosmic Costco or Akashic Records, I had been more of a jazz musician. Metaphorically speaking.

What I mean is, I had picked a few items—like abandonment—and in each lifetime, I bent it, twisted it, inverted it, and took turns beating it into submission and being beaten by it. A jazz musician takes a musical riff and does the same thing. And like jazz, it's the space between the notes where the real magic is found.

Yeah, I'm a freakin' poet.

Seriously, bro, I feel these things are just not exceptional anymore. When I can get on the Internet or surf hundreds of cable TV stations, I can find a dozen stories on all of the aforementioned rabbit holes. We are coming to a point where there are very few mysteries left in the world. Granted, while these are not common dinner conversations, they no longer have the required dress code of a straitjacket and tie.

Still interested in my story?

OK, then let me try to piss off your sensibilities.

While what I previously stated is all good stuff, I saved the best for last. People are nearly always interested in hearing about my NDE. That is, until I tell them I saw God—and it was George Carlin.

Yes, *that* George Carlin.

Dude! You say it's cool, but there are those who get pissed off something fierce.

The NDE paradigm is so sacred to some that just speaking of it is problematic. To equate the Master and Commander of the Universe to the comedian who gave us the "seven words" is sacrilegious. The Seven Last Words of Christ, they ain't.

Some people hate me immediately, dude.

This is especially so when you realize the currently accepted theory is, "You see who you need to see." I did not see the Christian version of God, Quan Yin, Jesus, or Muhammad. I saw the comedian George Carlin. In some NDE circles, I immediately discredit myself.

Why? Because my story does not support the traditional Judeo-Christian paradigm. Hell, it doesn't support anyone's religious paradigm.

OK, let me say it this way. When you run a nonprofit NDE group, you must speak to the masses with disposable incomes. My story offends some sensibilities and some wallets. So in those NDE circles, I am persona non grata. I'm in the fringe with the straights, and I'm in the fringe with the 'parastraights'. I'm weird all over, dude. I am an exile in my own land.

Yes, I am my own paradigm…and I own my paradigm. I don't know another person who has experienced all of these exceptional expressions of human potential. But, as I said before, I do not let my entire story out at one time…nor to any one person.

I usually stick with my NDE story because it is my story; my reality. It was how the message came to me, and I am not going to lie about it to make others feel comfortable or so that it fits conveniently into their familiar paradigm. The decades I have spent conforming with other people's comfort levels has gone from an irritating mosquito bite to a rusty cheese grater on my ass.

Agreed. Screw 'em. Cheers.

Honestly, between me and you, George Carlin as God would explain some of the hilarious and twisted memes that masquerade as truth in this world. Have you been to a Walmart at 2:00 a.m.?

Enough said.

So, you still want to hear this story?

I'm not sure how best to sum up half of a lifetime of both the strange and the familiar; I will do the best that I can. However, I believe I can promise you in earnest that this will not be a boring ride.

Fine. Here, have a cigar.

Well, if you like Arturo Fuentes, you will love this Rocky Patel Cameroon. Seriously, I have never had a bad cigar from them. Hell, I've never had even a mediocre cigar from them.

Excellent! Someone put Buffett in the playlist.

We've got our drink on, our smoke on, and good music. Are you ready to buckle up, buttercup?

All right then...once more unto the breach. Cheers.

Guitars, Cigars and Tiki Bars

CHAPTER 2

God whispers to us in our pleasures, speaks in our conscience, but shouts in our pains: it is his megaphone to rouse a deaf world." - C.S. Lewis

So, let's start this journey with something easy…ghosts. This story is where I met my first ghost and began my metaphysical journey.

Nah, it's not scary; it's endearing.

There was a time when I hated God insofar as any nine-year-old could. If you have known any nine-year-olds, you know they can get pretty worked up when the need arises. When my best friend died, I got worked up. When I realized I had contributed to his demise, I was pissed.

Hell yes, I was pissed! That prick, God, took something precious from me. So I took something away from Him; I took away my adoration.

I know. It sounds like something a grade school Hammurabi would have come up with during recess, but it's what this good Catholic boy had to work with at that age.

Guitars, Cigars and Tiki Bars

It started with my grandpa.

Back then, without an attached surname, the word "grandpa" meant something almost magical. Grandpa was my world. I was 4 years old and he was my hero with a thousand faces. He was my best friend, and as best friends do, we had many sacred rituals between us.

For example, we would drink our morning coffee together. I can still see the green Bakelite coffee cup in my tiny hand. He would occasionally read a noteworthy story aloud from the front page. I would return the favor regarding the antics of Snoopy or Jeffy from *The Family Circus.*

As I stood on the toilet, we'd both have our morning shave. His was the old-fashioned, cut throat razor and mine was a yellow safety razor sans blade. We lathered from the same Old Spice cup and prickly boar's hair shave brush. I skipped the Hai Karate aftershave.

He was my first partner in crime as we stole Archway iced oatmeal cookies from the cookie jar. He would enjoy his with his ever-present cup of coffee while I licked the frosting off mine before scarfing it down. At home, I would be scolded for such behavior. Grandpa created a space where I could be me.

A valuable skill I learned from Grandpa was how to effectively feign sleep when Grandma came in to check on us. If we were awake, she would have chores for us to do. The trick is to take deep breaths but don't over sell it.

You're right. Good skill to have as an adult, too. Some lifelong lessons are mastered before kindergarten. He was my—mentor—my Sherpa. He made imaginary things real.

I can still see Grandpa sitting on the back porch in his metal chair with a rounded back. It was that eggshell blue color—the one that came and went during the 1950s. Grandpa shared with me his love for nature and gardening. He would gaze out into his backyard, his focus occasionally drawn toward the birds in the large walnut tree that dominated the landscape. The look on his face, though, told me he was listening to a voice that only he could hear.

Grandpa was born in 1900. He wasn't a curmudgeon, but he regarded things that had no use as a waste of space.

He always had something in his hand: the newspaper, a hammer, a pocket knife. Most of the time, the "something" included a coffee cup. Other times, it was a cigarette he had rolled earlier.

Nah, he wouldn't have used a cell phone even if they had them back then. Well...maybe if you gave him a smart phone but introduced it to him as an electronic level and tape measure that just happened to include a phone, then he might use it.

Oddly, I did not think of him being in his early 70's. He was my friend—and I believe there is no ageism in true friendship.

When you are a child, you really don't know your place in the family. Having someone who is your second cousin, once removed, doesn't really make any sense. At that age, the world breaks down into people you can play with and people you can't. I had two cousins when I was growing up—Mark and Denise. What this meant in my four-year-old brain was that I had two people I could play with. Being an only child, that was important.

Yes, there were other people in my world called cousins. I was told they were family, but they lived too far away for me to get to know them. In my mind, they just weren't real cousins.

To my way of thinking, that made Grandpa just another cousin. After we had our morning coffee, we would watch TV. I still remember episodes of *Lassie, The Lone Ranger, Rin-Tin-Tin, Bonanza, Petticoat Junction,* and *F Troop.* Those were the best of times and they are the earliest memories I have of Grandpa.

In that same time frame, I also have a memory of Grandpa's razor strap on the back of the bathroom door. That was not something you ever wanted to meet. I met it, though.

I disappeared once while Grandpa napped.

Dude, he beat me like a rented mule.

There were two other people in my world during this time. Across the street lived Mrs. Collins and next door lived Mrs. Codington. They were grandma-like figures, as they were older, had white hair, and were kind of pokey. But they gave good hugs and nearly always had a cookie or two.

No, it did not occur to me that they were not family. I was happy to visit them and to hear their stories, and they liked having fresh ears to hear them. I thought I was hanging out with friends. Grandpa called it "making my rounds."

One time when Grandpa was asleep and I was not, I went next door to Mrs. Codington's. She was awake and she had cookies; that was all I required. I am sure the question was asked, "Does your Grandpa know you are here?" I don't know the answer I gave her, but I do remember her cookies. Fig Newtons. Never before had I experienced such a culinary wonder.

Well, at some point, Grandpa came over to get me and he was not very happy. He grabbed my hand and marched me back to the house. He led me into the bathroom directly, closed the door, and pulled the strap off the hook. I had no idea what was about to happen.

Without explanation, he beat my backside and my legs. I remember being shocked that a friend would do this to me. When he stopped, he looked at me as though I should say something. I had no idea what to say so I reached into my pocket and I offered him a cookie.

He didn't say a word. He hung the strap back on the door then went out to the living room to watch TV. The next day Grandma explained to me that I was not supposed to leave the house without Grandpa.

After that day, I never left Grandpa…but he would leave me. First, in small ways. Then, in a big way.

The first time I remember Grandpa leaving me in a little way was when he fed the bear that lived under the garage.

You heard me right. The bear. Under the garage. Turns out the fallout shelter under the garage was an excellent place to keep a bear.

Sometimes, I would be in the backyard and Grandpa would have me "park it" at the top of the steps that led down to the fallout shelter. You see, Grandpa had a bear and it needed to eat. Also, it had a fondness for curious preschoolers.

As coincidence would have it, the bear lived in the same place where Grandpa fermented the grapes from the vines in the backyard. In Grandpa's small slice of Eden, he grew apples, cherries, strawberries, grapes, and walnuts. Being the wizard I knew he was, Grandpa had grafted a cherry tree limb onto an apple tree. A simple procedure for an adult but magic to a child.

So, Grandpa had a wide variety of fruit with which to infuse his wine. Grandma may have made jelly from these items, but it had to be a modest amount because Grandpa loved that damned bear. He took fruit and sugar down to it all the time!

Well, I found it peculiar that Grandpa would go down to visit the bear for such a long time. Even more peculiar was that when he came back, he'd be in such a happy mood. Bears were supposed to be scary.

As time went on, I became braver and sat on a lower step each time I parked my keister. In an attempt to manage my curiosity,

Grandpa occasionally growled while in the cave. I wasn't too afraid because after the growl would sometimes follow a snicker.

I was close enough to the entrance of the cave that I began to recognize the unique aroma of fermentation contrasted with the pungent smell of the earth. To this day, when I go on a wine tour, the aroma is a time machine. I immediately recall my first best friend, his imaginary bear, and a shared snicker that transcends time and place but not memory.

Cheers to Grandpa.

Another thing I remember very well was how proudly he would look at me when I rolled cigarettes for him.

No kidding. Grandpa would be whittling something with his trusty pocket knife and I was rolling his smokes.

My preschool vocabulary included Zig Zag and Bull Durham, dude. But, hey, it was the 70s.

They probably looked like desiccated worms adhered to the summer pavement, but in my mind, they were more akin to starched white shirts—bright, stiff, and uniform like soldiers ready for inspection.

It sounds like a good memory. However, when my best friend got cancer and the ascribed cause was the cigarettes I had made…it was the first of my many horrors and lessons to follow.

Yes, it sucked. It felt like my heart was being removed with a wet/dry vac.

Know this, brother. If you want a child to learn new vocabulary words, whisper them. Like murmured curses from wizened hags, I learned "metastasize," "PEG tube," and "esophageal."

The words and their associated images were frightening to me, but I would have done anything for my best friend. With tiny, trembling hands, I assisted with dressing changes, bed baths, and tube feedings.

Dude, when I first saw a beer bong, it reminded me of the contraption that Grandma and I had used to feed Grandpa. Kind of blunted the party atmosphere. To this day, when I see a funnel, I think of PEG tube feedings.

When it was determined that Grandpa was too sick to attend my First Communion, calls were made and I received my First Communion while standing next to Grandpa's chair in the living room. I remember getting a piece of the big wafer. I also remember Grandpa receiving Holy Communion, Anointing of the Sick, and Last Rites.

Shit, dude, there was so much "God" in the room, I was sure there would be miracles. After all, I got a piece of the big wafer. It should have been the holy version of Popeye eating a can of spinach.

Seriously, I thought that Grandpa would get better, I would get the dog I had been praying for, and Grandma would forgive me for writing on the white marble coffee table with red crayon.

Wrong, wrong, and wrong.

Grandpa died with much more dignity than I demonstrated after his funeral. In my childlike despair, I decided to punish God. From that day forward, I promised never to pray to that asshole ever again. It was one of many earnest promises I would make and fail to keep.

My life has taught me this: Broken promises, like unanswered prayers, are sometimes for the best.

One evening, Mom came into my bedroom to ask me if I had said my prayers. I told her I had not because I hated God now.

He had taken away my best friend and, for that, I had told God he could go to hell.

As you can imagine, this was a mule kick in the gut of my "shock and awe" German Catholic mother.

Since my mortal soul was in peril, Mom arranged for our parish priest to intercede the following week. With his dour expression and man-given authority, Father Fishfry sat at our garage sale kitchen table, and essentially told me to get over it.

Nope. I was not buying what that old fart was selling.

Out came the big guns. He brought the Old Testament God with him—you know, the one who tortured Job just to make a point? Biblical fear also came with a side order of guilt.

Duty to the Church was projected into the conversation. Father Fishfry was keen to leverage the fact that I had only recently received the sacrament of Holy Communion. With his authoritative tone, he closed his sermon with how thankful I should be. Not only had God taken my grandfather to heaven, but He had accepted an unworthy, snot-nosed sinner like me into the Roman Catholic fold.

Three sets of adult eyes looked at me across the kitchen table and awaited my response.

My response? "God damn God."

Have you ever seen an apoplectic fit? I did—then and there.

Well, it was better than getting "altar boy-ed."

Like many before me, my relationship with Catholicism is littered with teachable moments yet unfulfilled.

Sure, I'll drink to that. Got any loaves and fishes to go with it?

I love that miracle. Makes me think Jesus had OCD. Fish and loaves. Fish and loaves. Fish and loaves. And, he's the son of God so it's not like he's gonna get tired. Fish and loaves. Fish and loaves. Fish and loaves. One of the apostles probably had to ball tap him to get him to reset.

Anyway, after this theological intervention had gone awry, I had a very lucid dream. In this dream, I saw myself sleeping and I was awakened by Grandpa. He was sitting at the foot of my bed and patting my knee in his gentle, loving way.

Brother, it was like an episode of a telenovela. I had awakened from a horrible dream! None of this had been real! The funeral narrative was all an illusion!

No, I don't know if Germans have telenovelas, but you get the gist, right?

I reached out and he took my hand. With that connection, the waking reality came back to me and I started to cry. In my mind, I heard his soothing voice. He told me not to be sad because he was very happy where he was. He loved me and would always love me. Since he was in heaven now, the cancer would no longer burden him. The pain would no longer vex him. He would be able to eat real food again, and from heaven, he would be able to keep an eye on me. He told me to think of him as an extra guardian angel and that he would forever watch over me.

For a heartbroken child, it was a miracle.

I leaned over and gave him a big hug. I still remember the texture of his maroon wool sweater on my face, his familiar smell of tobacco co-mingled with the Old Spice shave soap I had given him for Christmas.

I didn't just cry...I wept. I wept the honest tears of a frightened child upon his shoulder.

Soon, I lay back down in bed. He pulled the blanket up to my chin, tweaked my nose as he used to, and walked to the bedroom door. Before he left, he asked me to not be mad at God anymore. I agreed and fell fast asleep.

Well, the shit hit the fan the next morning.

At breakfast, I was more chipper than usual. Mom asked if I was feeling better. Around a mouthful of generic frosted corn flakes, I told her I was. When she asked why, I told her I was happy because Grandpa came to see me during the night.

I think my mother crapped her polyester bell-bottoms when I told her that.

Of course, I wanted to tell this story! I wanted to shout it as far as my voice could carry! Death is an illusion! Our loved ones are still connected to us! O, Death, where is thy sting?

Sadly, her resolute compulsion to bottle and sell the status quo to me overpowered my exuberance.

In other words, I was SOL. My message would be incinerated within moments.

Still, that event planted a seed that would grow—the lack of nutrition in the form of parental support notwithstanding.

The rationale Mom handed me was that Grandpa was not a ghost because he was Grandpa, and ghosts were scary. I replied that Casper was a ghost and he wasn't scary. I was then told that ghosts are from the devil and Grandpa was not of the devil. I countered that there was also the Holy Ghost. That was when I was summarily dismissed to go clean my room and do poop patrol in the backyard.

Yeah, that's what usually happened, dude. I asked a bunch of questions; they got tired of answering. I was then charged with some transgression related to homework or daily chores. The beatings would commence and my curiosity was momentarily constrained.

For whatever reason, though, I didn't stop asking questions. I just changed my audience.

Were there other visits? Not with Grandpa. He just played a one-night stand. But I have had visitations from my other three grandparents, my great-grandfather, my parents, a college classmate, and a coworker's grandmother.

She was my first non-family visitor. If they know they can get through to you and that you can get a message to someone they know, they will come.

No, they will go away when you tell them to 99.9% of the time. Like persistent groupies, though, some get past security. Then you need to wrangle them before they get clingy.

Early on, I asked my ancestors to act as intermediaries. I would be trying to get to sleep, but I'd get chills, hear noises, and such. I shouted that no one was allowed in my bedroom. I then asked my deceased family members to provide crowd control. For the most part, it worked.

Yeah...um, I have pissed off a few ghosts, too. I have cleared homes and other spaces. I have helped those that had been lost to cross over. When I worked in a haunted mansion in Indianapolis, I was bullied by ghosts...so, I bullied right back.

Maybe they saw me as a target. A medium once told me that these spiritual activities leave an imprint on your aura. Ghosts see it and try to connect with you. What I don't know is if there is a change in the shape, size or color of your aura that calls out to them.

No. I won't go there. More specifically, I have interacted with nonhuman ghosts a couple of times without intending to and regretted it. Ghosts, I'm OK with.

Ghosts that have never been human...I do not mess with them. I contract that shit out. It's not in my toolbox.

Gonna make me say it, huh? OK, then—demons.

See? The word itself has negativity attached to it. You are adding a quart of gasoline to a smoldering fire. I don't want to feed it so I call them nonhuman ghosts. They are spiritual energies that have never received the human experiential tool kit.

It means that they just don't understand empathy, compassion, sarcasm, love...the human experience. What they do understand is negative energy, and they will stimulate the crap out of you in various ways to produce it; it's their food source. Sometimes, you have to laugh at them to make them go away. Sometimes. Other times, you gotta push back.

I've learned to push. Look, I've been doing this off and on for nearly 40 years. You do anything that long, you're gonna pick up some tricks.

If you've read about it in a book or seen it in a show about ghost hunting, I've done it. But I like to stick to low tech methods. Batteries are a food source, too. Electromagnetic fields , or EMF, like a well-used magnetron from a microwave, can also work. They run on 12-volt power so I used to carry a motorcycle battery.

I started ghost hunting as a skeptic and used my toys: a digital recorder for electronic voice phenomena or EVP, a laser thermometer, an EMF detector, motion-activated cameras and the like. It's funny, really. You spend a thousand dollars on doodads just to sit in a dark room for hours...and nothing happens.

Right. But when it does...Bazinga!

In certain ways, I think that people tend to hide behind the equipment. It's something to create a buffer between you and the experience. Kind of like a podium when giving a talk.

As a skeptic, I wanted all the tools. Through exposure and discernment, I crossed over to believing. Now, I have a pen, paper, a candle and lighter, and a compass.

Well, I am less focused on proving the existence of ghosts and more interested in hearing the message they want to convey. With a compass, I can get all my binary questions answered.

Binary—yes/no, male/female. Set your compass facing north. Say aloud that east is yes and west is no. Then, you're off to the races. They move the needle as needed.

"Fun stuff" would include the odor of flowers, tobacco, perfume, and flatulence. Seeing toys maneuver themselves, a helium balloon ascending and descending—these are the anecdotes I call my Halloween stories. At that time of year, people love a good ghost story.

"Bad ones?" Murders—especially where the victims were children. Suicides inspired by possession. Ghosts of murderers who have no remorse. Former occupants of turn-of-the-century insane asylums. Nonhuman energies masquerading as humans you once knew.

Dude, like I said, I've been doing this off and on for almost 40 years. If you're a plumber for 40 years, you're gonna wrangle some turds. If you're an electrician, you're gonna get shocked. If you go looking for things that go bump in the night, you're gonna find them.

Yes, seriously.

That's why Ouija is so dangerous. You're creating a door to an unknown place and then inviting something in.

It's all fun and games until Sauron comes through. Then, the shit gets real.

By the way, have you noticed that the All-Seeing Eye looks like a flaming butthole?

Ha! Sorry, dude. Here's a napkin.

Hey, I'm a nurse. I've seen things. Weird things…abnormal things. And that was just at a family reunion!

I don't do ghost hunts anymore. It has become more of a tourist attraction than a labor of curiosity and compassion. People generally want the "boo" experience. They don't care about the message the ghosts are trying to convey nor do they care about helping a ghost to cross over.

Yeah, there are much more interesting things in this world than the people who have come and gone.

What have I learned? A lot, actually. But it all started with my visitation from Grandpa.

The lesson I learned from that incident was that when my parents answered my questions, I needed to question their answers. When other authority figures answered my questions, I began to question their authority. Just like George Carlin did. Like he once said, "I was a practicing Catholic until I reached the age of reason."

By and large, I see this as the point when my life path diverged from the cultural norm. And let's be real here—cultural norms are dictated by religions, politicians, and the media. They are the unholy trinity of population zeitgeist management.

To butcher some Shakespeare, it's all illusions told by idiots, full of sound and fury, signifying nothing but noise.

Deep shit, indeed. But, like Bill Hicks said, "It's just a ride."

It doesn't matter whether it was real or imagined. Like taking a placebo, it still had an effect.

I believe it was the ghost of a grandfather easing the anguish of a grandson which then planted the seed of rabble-rousing in the fertile mind of a child.

Yes, thank God for unanswered prayers.

Guitars, Cigars and Tiki Bars

CHAPTER 3

"Fighting for peace is like screwing for virginity." – George Carlin

How's that cigar? Like smoking a stick of butter, right?

You know, there's a restaurant outside Ybor City—The Columbia—where they still make cigars by hand and even use hundred-year-old wooden presses.

You have to go, man. It's a trip in Mr. Peabody's Wayback Machine.

I think it's beautiful! Picture pre-Castro Cuba. Parchment white stucco walls inlaid with hand-painted ceramic tiles, marble floors peppered with wooden tables and covered in starched white linen, black iron worked chandeliers that really were hand-wrought, stalwart wooden balustrades with carvings of Bacchus and his agents of revelry gazing upon you from the stairs and landing. Wherever you look, you get the sense of industry and passion. It's an experience I think everyone should have.

That's an interesting association; I think we all need our own St. Peter's Basilica—just not necessarily religious. More like a testament to what a person can achieve when passion, talent, and industry intersect.

Seriously, though, it could be a religious experience. Mojito starters, a great dinner, an hour of Latin-inspired dancing, and a world-class cigar. Life doesn't get much better than that, my friend.

So, what shall we talk about now?

Astral projection? Really?

Ha! Good for you! No tiptoeing here. Just jump in and make a splash! I like your style.

Let's roll like a Big Wheel.

So…do you remember how excited you were the first time you discovered folded money while doing the laundry? It's winning the redneck lotto! And, since I made a lighting rig for my pickup using duct tape and a discarded bowling trophy, I proudly consider myself "an honorary redneck." A country boy can survive, right?

Too young for that reference? Meh. Google it later.

One of the things that can bring you happiness in this lifetime is money found. Money found is better than money earned. However, like a magic trick, you shouldn't think about it too hard because you will eventually realize that the money was yours to begin with…and you're still stuck doing the damn laundry.

The only thing that would make it better is to be doing laundry for someone else and discovering money. Please take note that I do not condone rummaging through a stranger's laundry at the local laundromat. Phone calls will be made.

Just sayin'…

The excitement of found money is the best way I can explain how I feel when I go to garage sales. As some TSA agents know, one can find all sorts of delightful treasures while rummaging through other people's belongings.

Yes, I went there! Cheers!

Garage sales have given me some wonderful discoveries: an original Beatles White Album with photos, a first edition of Sigmund Freud's *Theory of Psychoanalysis*, and a 1960s Gibson electric bass guitar with an aftermarket whammy bar.

One summer day, I was exploring my neighborhood looking for something to do. I had recently acquired a 10-speed racing bike and was riding it like a hyperactive teenager. I shot past a house where they were having a garage sale and turned around when my curiosity overtook my need for speed. There were no records so my next target was a box of books. I bought the lot for three bucks. In retrospect, this wasn't just a deal. This was the hand of Providence.

Three books in particular captured my attention: *Silva Mind Control* by Jose Silva; *Far Journeys* by Robert Monroe; and *Illusions* by Richard Bach. These books captivated me immediately and have remained among my favorites for more than 30 years. Without a trace of hyperbole, I can say these books altered the trajectory of my life.

An example?

Well, before I had my learner's permit for driving, I was projecting my consciousness into my friends' homes.

No, I'm not shitting you.

I'm not sure how I did it. I just did it. It was easy once I learned there was a place between "awake" and "asleep."

Looking back, I think it seemed easy to me because no one was there to tell me that I could not do it—with the connotations of both permission and capability. I lived in an Indiana farm town but went to school in Indianapolis. When considering my friends were living miles away, and the frequency with which I was sent to my room, projecting myself there just seemed easier.

Well, of course...messing with my friends? Priceless. The rewards were worth way more than the effort.

I found one friend's porno stash. I found another's hiding place for weed. And for yet another, I found where his Dad hid his antique pistol.

It's just like an unused muscle. You know, like the one that wiggles your ears or nose. You have to discover it. Then, you need to exercise it. That way, you develop muscle memory. In astral projection, you can just go somewhere as quick as a thought.

It started with a beating by my dad. I was beaten with a belt and sent to my room for some transgression. After getting pissed off, I tried to imagine what my friends were up to. As I drifted off to sleep, I saw them having squirt gun fights with other kids in the neighborhood. I discovered later that it had been true.

On later occasions, I saw what friends were getting for Christmas, and that one had a Playboy hidden in his eight-year-old brother's room. I also discovered the same kid had an affinity for his mom's silk underwear which he had snuck out of the laundry hamper.

Paging Dr. Pull...Dr. Eddie Pull.

Man, it was funny, gross, and amazing all at the same time. And talk about positive reinforcement! He was stunned that I knew, but he thought his brother had told me. That summer, his nickname was "Phervé."

Why, yes, there was a girl in my neighborhood I crushed on.

No, I didn't.

No, I really didn't.

For one, I was 14. Two, I was still a "good" Catholic boy. Three, naked women scared me. Hell, in some ways they still do.

Dude, I didn't lose my "V" until I was in my third year of college. That was when I decided for good that I was not going to be a priest.

HA! Close your mouth, dude. You look like a drunk PEZ dispenser!

Yes, I thought long and hard about becoming a priest.

Something else long and hard made me change my mind. Hey-oh!

I had given it a lot of thought because I met the opposite of Father Fishfry…Father Cosmos.

Actually, he was humble in spite of the name.

Most of my grade school summer vacations were spent riding my bike to church so I could be a server for the daily Mass. Father Cosmos let me wear shorts and a t-shirt under my vestments. He let me eat unconsecrated wafers. It was his way of inserting humanity into a religious paradigm.

Contrary to what my father preached, Father Cosmos said it was OK to be "bad." He used a different word, though—nonconformist. I wasn't sure what it meant but it sounded cool. My parents were not thrilled with the influence, but they stayed mum as that was the summer I also read Webster's Unabridged Dictionary from cover to cover.

But the real motivation was the way Father Cosmos explained things to me. Those conversations started me on the path toward the understanding that having faith is better than belonging to a religion. He showed me that I could be a good person while not playing for any particular team. I later discovered he, too, was a nonconformist.

One amazing thing he did was pay a reduced portion of his taxes—and then he wrote sermons about his acts of civil disobedience!

Well, it was something Jesus knew a thing or two about, right?

Father Cosmos wrote a letter to the IRS stating that he did not support the military-industrial complex and, therefore, he would only pay the remaining percentage of his taxes.

No, it did not go over well, but he focused a bright light on an issue that many people—even now—do not even begin to think about, much less acknowledge. He used his station to illuminate injustice, to draw attention to things that were uncomfortable truths, and he took a stand that caused people to wake up. He was also newly ordained so he was flush with ideas and concepts inspired by Vatican II and the ending of the Vietnam War.

I guess you're right. He was a hippie priest. And I guess free love was part of that, too.

No, no buggering. At least not me…but I was an ugly kid. However, he did end up leaving the priesthood, got himself an MSW and a wife, and continued his crusade in other ways.

Funny, now that I think of it…in school I had a Catholic Father, Brother, and Sister—all of whom were part of my early childhood education—and they all left the ministry. And, oddly enough, they surfaced again in my Catholic high school. Maybe it was me?

Ha! I guess they just gargled the Kool-Aid but didn't swallow.

I think I'm lucky to have seen, so early on, that you can disagree with a dogma but still be a good person. I wanted to be a good person...so I did not go looking for naked women when I was projecting.

Well, college was another story.

Let's just say that the girl's dorm was not what I was expecting.

What can I say? HBO set some unrealistic expectations for me. I was expecting them to wear makeup when they went to bed. And Victoria's dirty secret is that she wears her older brother's t-shirt, with chili stains on it, to bed.

One summer, I worked in the Maintenance Department of the college. One of the tasks was to refresh the dorm rooms with new paint and resurfaced floors. I would have a series of rooms I could access and obtain proof of my astral projection. Most were empty...but not all.

No, it was a coed Catholic college, but it was still predominantly women. And being in the girl's dorm was definitely taboo. But there was the occasional discovery that stimulated my...curiosity. That's when I discovered I had a problem with poverty, chastity and obedience.

Dude, it's a trigger that can't be unpulled.

I'll say this. There are women out there who should be spies and actors because they are really good at hiding their L-card.

Others were equally good at propping up their V-card status. From one perspective, it looked like it was hermetically sealed in a Duke's mayonnaise jar. From another perspective, it was hit more times than a baseball trading card in bicycle spokes.

Yeah, don't give me 72 virgins. Give me 72 women who know what they want and also know how to give a man what he really wants…regular reinforcement and constructive criticism…and a Krispy Kreme donut.

See! We *can* follow directions when needed. Cheers!

So, let me backup a bit.

Astral projection, remote viewing, self-hypnosis, and intentional lucid dreaming are all different rungs on the same ladder of consciousness. Whether this ladder actually belongs to Jacob, I cannot say. I *can* say that I have walked on many of these rungs and each had its own degree of physical dissociation. If you want to dig into this subject a bit more, I'd recommend reading about Saint Jerome, King Solomon, Edgar Cayce, Project Stargate, and the lucid dreams of Generals Patton and Schwarzkopf.

I know, right? Hashtag mind blown.

Dude, there is *so* much more out there in the world…and now that the Internet has some of this knowledge in worldwide distribution, it can stagger the limits of one's imagination. It also means there is a shit-ton of detritus you need to wade through because every assbag with a computer and an opinion or agenda can muddy the waters.

Look up Emanuel Swedenborg! He was an 18th century dude who was one of those "everything" guys: mathematician, chemist, philosopher, musician…the dude farted science.

He openly talked about getting into a hypnotic state, astral projecting out into the Universe, meeting with benign entities of superior intellect, and then bringing that information back. You won't read that in any history book in school!

Again, no, I am not shitting you! Look it up! And the crazy thing is that his works are still available. Tesla was doing the same thing 200 years later and look at how much of his stuff is out there for the public to see.

Holy hell! The guy gave us radio, radar, wireless devices. Ever heard of ELF, HAARP, or transmitting electricity using rock strata rather than power lines?

All this was in the early 1900s and, yes, it staggers the imagination. Can you imagine how much of Tesla's work was deemed classified and remains hidden? Think about what the "Top Secret" reality is right now. I read somewhere that the computers we had as consumers in 1996 were available to the military in 1965. Honestly, I think there is a subset of the human race that lives in a technological world far superior to ours.

The earliest example I can think of is Leonardo DaVinci because he has gaps in his history where he just disappears. There are stories of him going into a cave and vanishing. And when you look at his works, there are subtle inferences to extraterrestrial influences. But don't take my word for it, look it up.

OK, back to projecting.

Living in the country, I was a bored, imaginative, and precocious latchkey kid. I wanted to find a pastime that did not include cow tipping or "mailbox baseball." That very mindset led me away from the rest of the neighborhood kids. Compared to astral projecting, what they were doing was stupid.

In my small town of three stoplights and 'the Kmart', I already had a reputation among the librarians. More than once, I was reminded that there were books in the library other than the ones about UFOs, ghosts, Harry Houdini, and the Bermuda Triangle. I finally acquiesced and read *Interview with the Vampire*. It was an "educational" read for this teenage farm boy.

Dude, that book was totally inappropriate for a 13-year-old. But my parents were just happy to see me toting around a nearly 400-page book.

Ah, right, the garage sale books.

The first of those books I tackled was *Illusions*. I read it first because of the unique printing. Episodic milestones within the story were marked with a departure from the typical book typeface and were replaced with an image of a dog-eared notebook page. Like pages from a diary, they contained meaningful insights to what the author was trying to convey through his characters.

Well, that, and the book's subtitle included the term "reluctant Messiah." It piqued my curiosity.

Well, J.C. did have a rough trip the last time he was here. I'm pretty sure his TripAdvisor rating of the Middle East would be NO stars. OK, maybe one star, provided it looked like the Star of David. *L'chaim!*

Silva Mind Control was in my hand a few times before I really opened it; my head was not ready for it. The term "Mind Control" did not sit well with me. That book sat on my bookshelf for nearly a decade.

Well, it didn't sit well with the public either. I'm pretty sure the title was introduced prior to any public knowledge of MK Ultra. Rather than *Silva Mind Control*, it is now known simply as *The Silva Method*. For those who can separate religion and metaphysics, it is a perfect platform for exploration.

In my mind, *The Silva Method* is a great framework for pulling together knowledge that would have been part of the esoteric mystery schools of previous generations. Also, there is no particular religion superimposed upon the information. In a country founded on repressive, patrilineal, Judeo-Christian moral values, it's refreshing.

I've taken the beginner BLS courses in Silva a few times as well as some others. I also learned about Psych-K from a Silva grad you may know of—Dr. Wayne Dyer.

You'd be stunned to know who some of the Silva grads are out there.

They're just like Canadians, dude. They look like us, they walk among us, but they're camouflaged...only until they want to talk "aboot" a hockey game.

Sorry, I didn't mean for you to snorkel your drink. Here's a napkin, hoser.

So, it was *Far Journeys* that provided the spark for my fire. In my mind, I had never encountered a book that took science fiction and presented it as 'science fact.' Robert Monroe presented something quite extraordinary but did so in a very matter-of-fact tone. It became a textbook for me. Perhaps "playbook" would be a better analogy. After a few tries, I realized the fiction wasn't fiction.

An early trip? One worth noting took place when in my early 20s. Many mental switches were being flipped on for me during those years: ghost hunting, psychic self-defense, psychometry, Tarot, and others. The ironic thing is I was going to school at a Catholic college in Indianapolis and the spirit activity there was off the chain. It was nearly impossible to *not* have some paranormal activity while I was on campus. I met ghosts, nature spirits, a couple of demons, and even discovered a few theater majors attempting a Black Mass in the school chapel.

Again, my childhood training of keeping my activities to myself was nearly always in my mind. But while I was there, I discovered remarkable stories about saints—St. Jerome in particular—who were able to bilocate or at least project enough of themselves to be recognized as a flesh-and-blood person. Some say it was due to their piety that they were able to do this. Maybe it was due to repetition, angelic intervention, alien intervention, or more easily done because of less EMF noise of modern society.

I was many things in my early 20s and being pious was not one of them. The select friends with whom I had shared my ability to astral project were nearly always confident that this was some sort of parlor trick. Telling somebody what he or she wore to bed, or some unusual items in the room, really had no effect on them. However, once I got to college, a couple of interesting variables were thrown into the mix.

Most of the people I met in college were new to me. There was no history from which I could draw like an ersatz psychic doing a cold reading. Secondly, except for one classmate in my "crowd", all were from towns far enough away that I could not drive to their houses, reconnoiter the area, and then come back to school the next day to make my report.

One evening a buddy of mine and I were hanging out at the girl's dorm. Someone suggested we play Euchre. A deck of cards appeared featuring pictures of naked men.

Like I said, dude, it was the girl's dorm.

One picture/card in particular was named Horst...and rightfully so. He would be the highest trump card regardless of suit. Soon, someone suggested we play "Strip Euchre." In the end, we all talked a good game, but did nothing more than talk.

Since getting naked was off the table, the discussion turned to other taboo card games and Tarot came up. I mentioned that Tarot was not just for fortune telling; it was a tool that could be used for many things.

Well, I shared that I had encountered paranormal trouble with a place I worked on campus, and had used Tarot to find out why the ghost in the house was so territorial. Using "ghosts" and "Tarot" in the same sentence made me about as popular as a bartender immediately following last call.

Emboldened by their enthusiasm, I volunteered the fact that I also projected myself into haunted houses.

Let me be clear. By projecting, I could see ghosts as they appeared in their lifetimes. More importantly, I was able to see them in the environment where they had lived.

Yes, seeing a ghost was amazing. But seeing a ghost in its environment—seeing things from their reality—was both frightening and fascinating. It was at this point in the conversation that I remembered my childhood training. I stopped talking and looked at the room.

They all looked like they had sat on their balls... metaphorically speaking... because, you know, girl's dorm.

They couldn't tell if I was full of crap, but they were genuinely curious. So we all agreed to devise a test where I would go to one girl's house that night. I would not say which one as my description had to have enough evidence to make it apparent to the listener. Once there, I would then look around the house to find something unique, and then report my findings to them the next day in class. That night, I got into bed and set my intention to go to the target house. It was approximately three hours away by car; I was there in about three minutes.

I entered through the back door which I thought was curious. Turns out, no one uses the front door. When I stepped into the house, I saw the kitchen immediately to my right and a set of stairs leading downward. I decided to start at the bottom and work my way up. As soon as that thought occurred to me, I was immediately at the bottom of the stairs. The basement was essentially rectangular, and I found myself in the middle of a long room. Because basement stairwells are usually located in a corner, they have the support of two walls instead of just one. A central stairway was odd, so I noted it. Looking around, I saw ordinary things like a couch, a throw blanket, end tables, and a sewing machine. Nothing really stood out.

With my next thought—that I needed to find something unique—my nose was immediately in front of and almost touching one of the basement's short walls. It was pickled, wood grain paneling. There was a door just left of where I was standing, but I did not open it. What captivated me was a very small window about five feet up from the floor. Although I am 6'5", it was directly in front of my nose! The opening was about the size of a holiday greeting card, and the paneling that had been cut out was put back into the same place. Around the opening was matching gray framing, as though it were an actual window. I chuckled. I felt like I was in the middle of an Escher drawing. It made absolutely no sense to me. I took a quick pass through the house, but there was nothing of note. I snapped back immediately to my home, gave my butt a scratch, and went to sleep.

The following day I met with both girls who had issued the challenge in the lobby of their dorm. I told them I had projected and began recounting the things I had seen upstairs. Neither one of them was impressed; a three-bedroom, two-bath, ranch-style home is unremarkable. Then, I got to the basement.

Reading facial expressions can be a subtle art form, but there was no special skill needed to read those two faces. While one girl looked confused, the other was wide-eyed and her mouth gaped open so wide that I could see the fillings in her back molars.

Yes, like a drunk PEZ dispenser. Cheers, again!

By far, the most stunning find was the tiny window in the wall. As it turned out, her father had quite the film collection, and behind the unopened door was a storage area and projection room. On movie nights, her dad would remove the small panel and project the movie directly onto the opposite basement wall.

I guess you're right; we're both projectionists. Good one!

Over the years, I have come to realize that my projections were initially an exploration into a world that few knew about. Later, it was a means to go someplace where it would be unsafe or unwise to go in physical form. There were also times when it was a survival technique.

What do I mean?

Regardless of your age or station, there are times when you just want to get away from it all. As an abused child, learning how to astral project was another way of doing just that. It was cheaper than going to the movies. It was healthier than taking drugs or alcohol. It was also a way to bend the rules. And I am absolutely a rule bender.

Being sent to my room meant that my physical body needed to be there. But, in my mind, I was visiting friends, family, going to parks, and exploring places that were both here and now. It was also a way to stick it to my dad who stuck me in my room.

I said "here and now" like that because, later, I began going places that were not "here" and not "now." I'll circle back to that.

Circle back to it now?

You sure?

OK...here we go. I would combine my interest in ghost hunting and my aptitude for astral projection to scout out the place beforehand.

Not really location scouting, per se. Granted, the shows you see on TV are heavily edited. I can't tell you how many hours I have spent sitting in the dark and having absolutely nothing happen. Most of the time nothing happens.

No, that's *not* a good thing when you are looking for ghosts. You *want* something to happen. That's the point, bro.

Let me put this another way and describe it from their perspective. Let's say you are powerless to let people know you're in your home. Hell, they can't even see you. One day, several people barge in and start waving around weird and futuristic equipment. It would be scary. So, since you can't control who comes in, you would opt to hide or lay low until they went away. Or to scare them off.

Ghosts are people, dude. They just don't have a physical body anymore. They have likes and dislikes, fears, hopes, and predilections.

Look at it this way, if you were an ass in this life, you will probably be an ass in the afterlife. So, too, if you were a loving caregiver, a comedian, or a protector. In many respects, not much changes personality-wise.

Initially, I started checking out areas where I'd be investigating the following evening. I wanted to find the "hot spots" so I wouldn't be bored. My first time projecting in, I immediately discovered that they could see me. Most knew that my projection was neither a ghost nor a human. In fact, they were curious how a human could behave as my projected self did. "You move like we do," was the thought that entered my mind most often, so I would just continue the conversation from there.

Just good manners, you know. Hi, I'm John. I'm an investigator. I'm with a team that will be here tomorrow evening. I will look different as I will be here in physical form. The team will be looking around and recording our discoveries. We will only be here for a couple of hours. You are welcome to visit with us or to ignore us.

It was pretty cool as I got more EVPs than most. I also discovered that ghosts of children would play with me.

I would bring a doll or toy. Sometimes a ball...things that a child from a century ago would recognize as a toy. Something that would not be intimidating.

If I brought a zombie doll or a light saber, I'm not sure what they would do with it. Most times a flashlight was interesting enough, but a ball or a balloon would nearly always elicit signs of interaction. Especially if it was a helium-filled balloon.

Think about it though...the people there are...well, people. If I brought a doll to a place I know a little girl has been seen, then I would probably get a reaction. If I brought it to an abandoned prison, then probably nothing would happen. If I was going to an abandoned prison, I would probably bring a bottle of whiskey, a Vargas pin-up girl, a deck of cards, or a set of antique keys.

Yeah, the same things you'd want to interact with if you were stuck in a prison for 20-to-life and it became eternity.

That's a good question. Are they trapped there for eternity? I don't have an answer. But, I suppose that free will still exists. I think they could leave the prison if they wanted to. Just as with living folks, most restrictions are mentally imposed, not physically imposed. Just like my emotional childhood triggers, they seem to be physical limitations, but really are mental ones.

Nah, I think physical abuse reinforces the mental abuse. I bore no ill will toward my Grandpa when he got me with the belt. His philosophy toward childcare was if you don't listen, you're gonna feel. With my dad's belt, it was different. It wasn't that he enjoyed it. I think, though, he transferred his aggression from other life situations into my whippings.

Well, my parents are dead, so I can't ask them in this reality. But I have had the discussion with them from the other side. I did not get words; I got emotions. There was a splash of remorse for the pain they caused, but it was immediately countered with a tidal wave of love.

I think, broadly speaking, the physical abuse was due to the fact that I did not conform to their expected behavior. When they didn't have the compensatory strategies to deal with their own frustrations, they went with what they knew. I mean, when my dad was a kid, he painted the dog. If I painted my dog, there would have been a frame of reference. Talking to the dead, and the other tidbits I demonstrated, were beyond their ken. They fell back on the familiar.

OK, let me add some woo-woo to the same thought. They did what they did because I asked them to do so.

What I learned while exploring my own abuse, and its metaphysical cause and effect, was what I would later come to know as the "Sacred Wound."

The Sacred Wound. It is part of several American Indian philosophies.

It does sound sort of strange, but hear me out.

Before we are born…when we choose the lessons we want to learn this time around…we select the figures who will inflict that spiritual wound. In the case of the Sacred Wound, it requires the gravitas of a parental figure. This injury will serve as our prime mover. It will motivate us to survive the future trials necessary to succeed in our overall spiritual mission. In medicine, we call it therapeutic trauma.

A surgery is therapeutic trauma. Debridement of a wound is therapeutic trauma. A root canal is therapeutic trauma.

Brother, I can't overemphasize the power of this realization. When you become aware that your earthly circumstances are of your own design, and that your life is part of a much greater design, you can no longer place the blame of the wound on your parental figures. Or on anyone else. They are simply honoring your spiritual contract.

Finding an external target for our woes is both deceptively easy and usually incorrect.

No one wants to admit to pissing on their own boots.

Look, I could grind on and on about what mean parents I had… and the decades long abuse… and the cruel circumstances in my life. We all could do that; everyone has been bullied at some point. Everyone has been Mr. Rabbit. I can fix the blame on my tormentors, or I can fix the blame on their parents who also abused them. And on and on.

On the other hand, I can accept responsibility for my life lessons—for both my body and soul—and rejoin the growth process that Earth provides. If you feed the victim mentality too long though, it becomes part of your identity and you get too attached. Then you're really screwed and end up paying for your therapist's new Range Rover.

Dude, they love you enough to inflict that wound. For example, no one in their right mind would stick a needle the size of a coffee stirrer into a two-year-old. But, if that two-year-old has pneumonia and is dehydrated, they need IV fluids fast.

Yes, I know it sounds crazy. If you lost a spouse, a sibling, or a friend to some tragic incident, you wouldn't want to assign blame to the victim. We're told it is never the victim's fault…and on one level of reality, I agree. On another level — the greater one, the one devoid of emotion and human ethics— the rules change.

Yes, I know some people will never accept it… while in this lifetime.

Agreed. It will be one of the hardest lessons to accept. But I guarantee, once you do, it is one of the most liberating human experiences you will ever know.

Yes, you can curse me now…and, hopefully, thank me later.

Guitars, Cigars and Tiki Bars

CHAPTER 4

"I'm not quite dead yet!" – The Holy Grail

How's your drink?

I had never been much of a Scotch person until I encountered a blended Japanese whiskey from Suntory called Hibiki. It sounded so absurd that I just had to try it. And, brother, it was amazing. I swear I could taste apple, smoke, cinnamon, and Irish peat moss in that delicious amber mystery.

It made no sense to me…well, it makes as much sense as a Japanese bagpipe player. But, as I hope this will be your experience with my story, my curiosity was richly rewarded.

Ready to go another round?

You have been a kind and patient listener. Thank you. Sorry for my douchebaggery earlier.

So, which rabbit hole shall we go down now?

Alrighty then, let's have a go at the metaphysical elephant in the room. As I mentioned earlier, I had a near-death experience and, during my experience, I did not actually see God. Instead, I saw the comedian George Carlin.

Yes, *the* George Carlin.

No, he was not dead at the time. This was back in 2005.

No, I'm not saying God is George Carlin, but if that was the case, it would explain some of the crazy-ass shit going on around here.

No, I never wrote a book about it.

Because, it seems to be in the "cosmic playbook" that once you have an NDE, you are required to write a book about it. That expectation is why I refused. Some of those books suck, quite frankly. Also, it tastes too much like proselytizing to my palate.

Dude, if you want to get your "swole" on for J.C., that's fine with me. Just don't knock on my door and ask me to spot you. I got shit to do.

When those people come to my door on a Saturday morning asking if I found Jesus, I tell them I never knew he was missing, and close the door.

OK, sometimes I say I have my plastic Jesus on the dashboard, and that's all I need. Not too many people get that reference anymore, so the look they give me is priceless.

"Well, I don't care if it rains or freezes, long as I have my plastic Jesus…"

Go Google it.

First, there is an ongoing debate among the "Near-Deathers" on what actually constitutes an NDE.

No, I'm not kidding. Some say you have to have your heart stop. Others say you need to be declared dead. Still others say you need to stop breathing. I mean, the club is already exclusive enough, so the whole entrance criteria is bizarre to me.

The sad thing is some snapper-heads have committed real trauma and betrayal to NDE'ers by listening to someone's sacred story, and then denying its validity because it did not conform to their own narrow criteria.

Trust me, brother. I have heard it all from the naysayers: Why didn't you see Jesus? What's sacred geometry? Why a crystal snowflake? Why didn't they have wings? Why aren't you more holy? Shit, man. I've even been called a "metaphysical dick."

This is just a fraction of the crap I've had to shovel. Just because you have an NDE doesn't mean you come back farting glitter bombs and miracles.

Why me? I don't have an answer. If I was God and I wanted to convey a message to humankind, I would pick a messenger who was pretty, smart, famous…one of the "damn" people.

"Damn" people.

You know…the people who hit the genetic lotto. Those who get up in the morning looking like they just got out of the hair-and-makeup chair. They are so consistently, effortlessly stunning that you stop what you're doing, unabashedly stare at them and say…DAMN!

What am I? I'm the "six weeks picture." In any before-and-after pictorial, there is the six weeks pic. You can see something is going on, but you're not quite sure what it is. Losing weight, hair plugs, reassignment surgery, witness protection…it could be anything.

Maybe God decided to scatter the message more broadly. I mean, he sent one guy a while back…and things didn't go so well for him. Remember what I said before about his "TripAdvisor" entry? No stars.

Maybe the world has become more like a mass casualty. You send all the paramedics in the city and not just the local wagon. Rather than send one Messiah, you send thousands of people who demonstrate kindness and strength in challenging circumstances. They're here, if you look for them. A collective Christ Consciousness—if you will forgive the alliteration.

First, you never, never, never dismiss someone's pain in the moment. Period. Regardless of whether they nearly died, their dog died, or their favorite reality show—the Real Housewives of Jellystone Park—was canceled, that particular discussion is a heart-based one. You just hold sacred space and listen. Quantify it later when they are back in alignment.

No! I don't care if it was an NDE, a cardiac NDE, a respiratory NDE, or almost an NDE...this dipshit argument about who's kung fu is better than another's is the same divisive bullshit that we use to splinter our humanity and dilute our innate divinity.

That bullshit reminds me of religion, too.

For some self-appointed gatekeepers, I did not have a near-death experience because I never stopped breathing, or because my heart never stopped, or because I was not declared dead. For others, I did have an NDE because I had been on life support, in a coma, with multiple organ system failure. My awareness of some of my visitors during the coma seems to indicate that my physical and energetic bodies had not fully reintegrated. Hell, some people split hairs by saying I had an nNDE—a near Near-Death Experience.

No, I am not shitting you.

By some others' connotations, I had an STE—a spiritually transformative experience. Think of it as an NDE without the pesky "death" part. Pretty standard fare on the shamanic pathway. It's the western people who get their knickers in a twist.

Oh, it gets worse. There is also a small minority of meat suits who choose to invalidate my experience because I did not see Jesus.

I shit you not. It's like a group of doctors arguing about what kind of wound it is while the patient is bleeding out.

To borrow from Gandhi, I do not like your Christians as they are so unlike your Christ. If I offended any Christians, I hope they can be Christian enough to forgive me.

Anyway, I attempted to share my story in a few places where I did not conform to their expectations. So it was easier to move on rather than to force them to open their minds.

Refill? Sure. How about something with some levity? I'll do a Mai Tai.

Did you say garnish or garish?

Same thing, right? Absolutely! Bring on the pineapple wedge and the umbrella!

There's something else...a disclaimer before we go any further into this tale. When I was over there, communication was not through the five human senses. A more appropriate metaphor would be to say I was connected to all the Internet traffic in the world. When I made the connection with George, or Source, or God over there, it was a data download of energy. But the energy had emotional content...and a whisper of the infinite possibilities that could be.

I was able to discern the distinct energy of wisdom, knowledge, love, humor, and a dash of mischievousness. All of these wavelengths came together in my mind as though George Carlin delivered it. My response was met with happy approval and the show rolled onward. The rest of my experience was with George's image.

Since the common thought among NDE'ers is that we see who we need to see, I find it interesting that I saw George. Frankly, there wasn't anything humorous about my life at that particular point. In fact, it sucked. But I did recognize him as a sommelier of society's bullshit.

In early 2005, as was the case with many families, my family was struggling. My job was being outsourced to India, and the proprietary software I taught was becoming the software equivalent of BetaMax. I had made a promise to keep my family in place, but I was living in a place where I could not maximize my income. With both of us out of work, bankruptcy soon followed. I ended up going back to nursing school in an effort to change our fortunes. Well, I succeeded...just not in the way I thought I would.

Life is what happens when you are busy making other plans. Cheers!

So, I was working a part-time job, going to school full time, and had some responsibilities with a company my wife and I had started the year before. Since my wife traveled, I was also playing Mr. Mom to a spoiled teenager. To say I was burning the candle at both ends would have been an understatement. Add to that the facts that my daughter would not speak to me and I was sleeping in a spare bedroom without a bed.

I slept atop suitcases cobbled together to form a pallet.

Failing at nursing school was inevitable in my wife's mind. Guess she thought I didn't deserve a bed.

Well, we all have our demons. Some of us take longer to figure out all you need to do is stop feeding the beast. Or at least choose to feed something that is either better for you, or better to you.

Since classes were designed to keep the nursing student headcount low, missing class was not an option but rather grounds for removal. I sucked it up and went to class and clinicals with bronchitis and a fever.

Yes, nursing students as a vector for infection is ironical.

I started feeling profoundly sick a few days later so I took some immunity stimulants and Tylenol. I was determined not to surrender. I was not going to give my wife the satisfaction...and that is how a perfect storm began to brew. While my wife and daughter were on spring break, I wrote in my journal, "I wish I was in a coma until this is over."

Right. Careful what you wish for.

After several days of just grinding it out, I was exhausted—bone-tired as Grandma used to say. No amount of caffeine, nor countless little bottles of energy shots, could keep me moving. This marked my first surrender as I stopped trying to do it by myself and drove to the local clinic with an X-ray machine. Doogie Howser was holding down the fort that night at the local Doc-in-the-Box.

When he returned with my X-rays, his complexion matched his starched white jacket. My results? Whiteout in all five lobes. Or, for the nonclinical folks, pneumonia of a Schwarzenegger magnitude. Essentially, my lungs were bags of snot. I took my results and agreed to see my own doctor the next day... but I lied... just a little.

Dr. Doogie thought I was going to my family practitioner. Instead, I was seeing my endocrinologist; I had no idea whether she had so much as glanced at an X-ray since med school. She had. Also, as luck would have it, her husband was a well-known immunologist.

Brother, she flipped out! She called the hospital and directly admitted me over the phone. I agreed to go there immediately. OK, I lied again... just a little.

Before you get your man-panties puckered over my stubbornness, I had worked in hospitals long enough to know the food stinks and the coffee tastes like hot water stirred with a brown crayon. I went home and had a proper English breakfast, strong coffee, and a hot shower. Then, I made my way to the hospital. That's where things got fuzzy.

For instance, I don't remember my drive, but I do remember looking for a parking space. I don't remember how my wife got there, but I remember a guy in a white coat trying to explain what they were going to do to me. I remember my wife saying, "Do you understand?" Then, my second surrender... consciousness.

Other acts of surrender followed: independent breathing, kidney function, communication, even my humanity, as others spoke to one another over my body as though I did not exist. I was a medical curiosity because there was no clinical trigger for my illness.

Yes, I had pneumonia, but there was no bug...no virus. In spite of my exhaustion, fever, and pulmonary shock, all the lab tests came back negative. Scientifically, I had no reason to have pneumonia. Thus began my unplanned, two-week vacation coma.

In retrospect, I wish my journal entry had mentioned winning the lottery. To the staff, I looked like I was circling the drain.

> Patient is a married 39-year-old white male, morbidly obese, presenting with an altered LOC, productive cough with crackles and wheezing and self-reported fever of 102 F. Patient was directly admitted by his endocrinologist this morning who stated he has white out in all pulmonary lobes. Confirmed by x-ray in ER. BP 142/100, HR 100, Temp 103.3 F, O2 Sat 64%.

> Patient stated he drove himself to the hospital but does not remember where he parked. Patient LOC continued to fall during admission. A & O x 2. NC O2 @ 10L started while waiting for bed assignment. Wife arrived to complete history. Patient is in nursing school and is a former opera singer.
>
> Patient lost consciousness in ER bay and failed to respond to sternal rub. O2 Sat 60%. Tracheotomy was ordered but wife requested additional attempts to intubate to preserve vocal cords. Intubation patent 40 minutes post presentation. Working diagnosis of ARDS secondary to pneumonia. No living will or advanced directive on file. Chaplain notified.

Oblivious to the drama playing out around me, I was a stone skipping across the surface of consciousness in spite of the induced coma. I had episodes of consciousness that made no sense. I was seeing people I had not seen in months or years. Sometimes I'd see them from above as though I was a fly on the wall.

> Day 4: Patient continues to deteriorate. Efforts to clear lungs ineffectual via suction. Respiratory support is further complicated by decreased kidney output. Although WBC count is elevated, blood tests have come back negative. Antibacterial and antifungal IV meds administered prophylactically. Wife has requested Infectious Disease consult. Working diagnosis of ARDS confirmed.

As the parade of faces continued, their demeanor changed as they all exhibited grim expressions. I saw one family member hovering over me with a look of great concern. I had to be dreaming this, I thought, because she had end-stage lung cancer. I felt fine until she showed up. I knew something was going wrong at that point, though. Later, someone was asking me what music I wanted to listen to and I had headphones placed on my ears. I even had a visit from a high school friend with whom I had not spoken in several years. The weirdo was even holding my hand.

> Patient continues to deteriorate. Wife advised to notify family. Kidneys have failed despite Lasix therapy. Patient weight up 11 pounds to 377. Specialty bed ordered. Additional blood tests are negative. Need to rule out Legionnaires Disease.

It eventually dawned on me that I must be truly ill when my wheelchair-bound mother flew up from Florida. It was then and there I knew I was truly hosed. I would find out later when I floated over to the nurse's station that I had respiratory failure, kidney failure, and my heart marched to the beat of competing drummers.

> Day 5: Patient prognosis poor due to continued respiratory and renal system failures. Blood tests remain negative. Patient began showing signs of cardiac stress with random episodes of PVCS and sustained trigeminy. Patient weight 403 pounds. Third spacing present in all extremities, abdomen, and eyes. Patient is an organ donor. Emergency contact numbers are up to date.

Then...I started coming back on line after 13 days. On the surface, nothing had changed. Down where it mattered, everything had changed.

Gradually, the things I had surrendered came back to me. First was consciousness, followed quickly by my precious identity via finger spelling which I had learned during my Cub Scout years. I shifted from an object for possible publication to a living person with every shift change.

Man, it was a crazy time! I realized the scope of my fame as the parade of various physicians, specialists, technicians, and nurses poked and prodded me. Just as my clinical illness trigger was unknown, so, too, the reason for my equally dramatic turn around. The word "miracle" was mentioned more than a few times; my primary diagnosis was ARDS which kills half the people who get it. Twenty-eight days after my admission, I came home to pick up where I left off.

That's the black and white of my story. But something happened just after being removed from the respirator...something that stoked the embers of my soul. It's what gave me the courage to once again redirect the trajectory of my life. It would be the lifeboat for the storms to come. It's why I survived a coma, bankruptcy, divorce, welfare, and the death of my parents. It is why I am still here today. I've mentioned it before; I call it Obstinate Spirituality.

```
Day 12: Patient renal function has returned.
Between 0300 and 0530, patient urinary
output was 3 liters. Sinus rhythm since
0400. Will continue to monitor.

Renal function continues to be good with an
average of 1 liter per hour. Cardiac
function normal. Patient became
increasingly febrile during sedation
challenge. Max 102 F. Third challenge
successful. Sedation discontinued. Temp
101.1 F.
```

Here's where it gets funky.

I think it was the second night out of ICU and I couldn't get to sleep. Noise on the floor was too much for me. My nurse finally gave me diphenhydramine to help. I closed my eyes and tried several mental relaxation techniques. Around 2:00 A.M., I finally was able to sleep. Some of the thoughts flitting through my head as I drifted off were:

This is as close to Death's door as I can get without tripping, skidding, or stumbling over the threshold.

Between Reiki and Silva Method, I thought I had a good "team" on the other side. Why hadn't I seen them?

I should have had an NDE.

And so...I did.

Holy shit, indeed.

I was in a void of blackness where my consciousness was no longer tethered to my body. Having traveled many times with astral projection, I was accustomed to the sensation of movement...of flying without any wind or friction. But this was different as I had no body. In this void, there was only my consciousness. Exercising understatement, I thought to myself, "This is interesting."

In a field of white, a speck of brighter light appeared in front of me. I could not discern if it was small and inches from my brow or a star millions of miles away. What I did know was that it was a fellow consciousness in this space. My thought was, "I wonder what that is?" and the accompanying intention was to be closer to it so I could find out.

Bang! It was immediately so.

I was now enveloped in this profound and complete whiteness. No words can convey my total satisfaction in this place. No hunger, no pain, no weakness, no petty human crap like back pain, an itchy foot, or body odor. The gross, leaky, meat sack we have to wear to be human was a memory falling into the distance. This was my true Self. This was...bliss!

"Who are you?" I thought.

"I'm everything," I heard in my mind.

Although the words sounded like my own voice in my head, I was most surprised by the carrier wave of emotional content washing over me. It was infinite intelligence with love, joy, happiness and, of all things, a bit of mischief. If I had a mouth, I would have smiled broadly.

Yes, that would be George. Years later, I stammered out this explanation to a colleague of mine. We both agreed that George Carlin as God would be decidedly cool. I still smile about this.

At this point, I was no longer forming words with George but expressing myself with mental intention. Frankly, words were just too damn cumbersome. They still are. Intentions, with a bit of emotion, were my words and punctuation now. At this point, I asked, "What is it you want me to know?"

A thin, silver cord of energy—or plasma—appeared between us. If I thought the previous carrier waves were intense, the direct connection to Source without any of the dissonance created by my residual humanness, was gloriously overwhelming. I now had context for the word "rapture." More than a decade has passed and it still brings me to tears.

Yes. I still miss it. The longing is diminished over time, but it never goes away.

Why? Because every negative emotion, trauma, experience, or detriment that has ever weighed me down in this lifetime is lifted as easily as you would take off a hat that no longer fits. The reconnection with Source awakens the sleepwalking soul, and any memory of *any* diminution falls away effortlessly.

Time passed. Actually, time does not exist there. It would be more accurate to say I went from a state of receiving information and becoming comfortable with it, to a state of being ready and willing to receive more. There was much more!

We were in a field of blackness now and I became aware of a snowflake. It was a crystalline, energetic structure that was finite...but quite ornate. I noticed that our energetic thread was also a part of the snowflake's structure. It hummed and pulsated as energy flowed throughout all of its intricate joints and angles. In its three-dimensional shape, it reminded me of some of the fractal artwork that has always fascinated me. It had patterns that repeat, patterns that overlap, and patterns that are identical except in ratio. It was as perfect as the spiral created by the Fibonacci sequence blended with a richly performed piece of orchestral music. It was geometric and harmonic perfection!

The carrier wave of energy/knowledge increased. I realized then that the other points of light within the structure were the consciousness of my family members! I immediately had emotional access to all of them. In fact, that was how I recognized them—by their vibrational frequency.

What seems interesting now that I am back, but presented as quite obvious while I was there, is that death is meaningless. Family members who had passed away had a vibrational intensity as strong as those who were still alive back on Earth.

Another memory is that I did not sense a slowing of the data rate as I was exploring my family member's emotions. I felt joy akin to that which is demonstrated by a puppy darting back and forth when a family comes home from a trip. I bounded back and forth checking out different vibrational rates. Perhaps this was an energetic way of just saying, "Hi!" And, though I tell you this story in a linear fashion, its occurrence was simultaneous and instantaneous.

The other thought I had was equivalent to the words, "Ah, I remember how this feels." Again, a period of reorientation occurred so I could tune back into Source. Another way of saying this would be that I needed to pause so I could return to the faster data rate in which Source communicated. I remember focusing my intention away from everyone else and back to Source. Once ready, my intention was, "Well, show me more."

The sky exploded! The curtain had been pulled away revealing the fractal pattern of the Universe. The snowflake was a mere cell of an enormous organism.

The data cascading into my head was the equivalent of someone moving from darkness to candlelight... to a flashlight... and then to a magnesium fire. The fractal crystalline structure grew exponentially. I saw my family, my friends, my acquaintances, my patients, everyone I would ever meet, everyone they would ever meet, every energetic exchange of all I had interacted with or influenced. Only for a moment, it appeared as a soccer ball before it became so complex that it would be easier to say it was a ball of crystalline fire. However, it would also be accurate to say that it was like an atomic structure because its volume was mostly empty space.

Source was still monitoring me as I extended my intention to random places. I was happily surprised to find a friend, a stranger, a tree, a rock, a new plant, another life form, another planet. Like I said, words are cumbersome, but they're the best I can do.

My thoughts could be summarized as this: You want me to remember that we are all interconnected. Friend, family, foe, tree, rock, planets, solar systems, galaxies, and so on. We are part of Source. Source is infinite and connected to all. Ergo, we're all connected to everything!

What followed, I cannot describe. Human words are as ineffective as trying to build a house with a Nerf hammer. My mediocre explanation is this. Take the feelings of unconditional love, joy, acceptance, forgiveness, and pride; add the words,

"YES! HE GETS IT!" Pour it all into a bath and then submerge yourself into that sexy satori stew for a thousand years.

The structure vanished and I was back where I started. Source and I were still connected by the beautiful silver strand. It began to stretch as Source pulled away. "Oh, I'm going back now," I thought, with no emotional content. Source continued to retreat until I opened my eyes to find myself staring at the 219 holes-per-tile that comprised the ceiling of my hospital room. According to the clock about 90 minutes had passed.

Like a person briefly awakened in the middle of a great dream, I repositioned myself around my pillows and O2 and IV lines, then took a deep breath like a free diver and went back to sleep. I wanted more!

This time I found myself in a sweat lodge. I had never been in one before, but I had heard them described. Judging from the terra cotta color of the sand beneath my feet, I would say I was in the southwestern United States maybe near the Four Corners.

The lodge was about five feet deep into Mother Earth with sandy stones embracing its circumference. Each stone was roughly the size of a large shoebox; they were stacked high enough so that while standing in the lodge I could not see out. Stark white deadwood, bleached clean by decades of desert sun, supported a thatched roof made from tied bundles of high grasses that grew in the area. A small bench had also been thoughtfully dug out so that participants could sit with their backs leaning against the earthen womb.

These details remain amazingly vivid. I think this is deliberate so I can still discern over here that the experience was not a dream. My dreams are typically two-dimensional. When they do have color, they are muted. This experience was definitely immersive. I remember the heat on my cheeks, the comforting smell of the smoke, the coarseness of the sand under my hands, and the crackle of the fire as it cheerily chewed through hardwood.

My perceptions were the equivalent of a fade-in camera shot. Or a dimmer switch being slowly dialed up to reveal the room's secrets. Finally, I became aware of an ancient Indian sitting almost opposite of me in the sweat lodge. He was the epitome of what I thought an Indian should be with a few feathers braided into his hair—not the war bonnet that old Hollywood oftentimes portrayed. He wore an open vest of some organic material, pants from animal hide and…damn, if he didn't have the same gregarious smile that George was so well known for wearing!

What was most striking to me were the lines upon his face. It was an ancient and yet ageless face. It was the countenance of wisdom.

Matching that grin were eyes that sparkled and shone forth with the same love, mingled with mischief, which I had felt earlier. Those eyes could have belonged to either a leprechaun or Santa Claus himself. But surrounding those sparkling eyes and loving grin was a face like a saddlebag left in the sun too long. Those long furrows left shadows on his face no matter where he looked. But I could tell he wore each one with pride. Well-earned badges of courage, perhaps.

We smiled at each other and, as I had done before, I spoke to him without words. I asked what I should call him. With twinkling eyes and a lopsided grin, he replied, "Joy…with Attitude."

Oh yeah. I was liking this guy.

During our conversation, the fire in the sweat lodge changed colors. In the beginning, it looked like any normal fire. However, throughout the course of our discussion, the flames changed to an emerald green. When I started asking questions about my soul group, the fire turned purple. Otherwise, it was a loving conversation between a pupil and student who had not seen each other in a long while. The comforting sense of familiar camaraderie was ever-present.

What ensued was a conversation that seemed hours long. Rather than subject you to dialogue, I will summarize:

We humans are spirits in a material world, and that world is meant to be a playground for learning.

We take ourselves too seriously—and do so too often.

We are both who we are and where we are by our own choices—by the things we have created and things we have allowed.

We are always connected to Source, but we usually focus on the operas of our lives rather than on Source.

Everyone has the capacity to be awake / psychic / in touch with Source. It merely requires choice.

There are people here who are awake and people who are asleep. Some of the awakened are in learning mode. Some are in refinement mode.

Some of us here at this time are spiritual "paramedics." Those who are asleep are going to struggle to remain in that state. Some will awaken. In short, some will not awaken. Assist - Do not persist.

Everyone has a team of helpers in the spiritual realm. Some are specifically for you; some are for when you require specialized help.

Practice love and forgiveness at every opportunity—but start with yourself.

That's it.

OK, yes, there was more. Other information was imparted to me that I am not yet ready to surrender. Some of it was specifically for me. Not so much warnings as navigational signposts.

I had a very long and painful road ahead of me at that point, including divorce, betrayal, various physical injuries, professional sabotage, and a parent's suicide.

Yeah, it's a lot, but I've always been an overachiever.

Seriously though, we're back to the stressor question. Some of these issues were on par with losing my lunch money. Others...not so easy. Any of those aforementioned life events are capable of breaking a person, but each one was also an echo of an earlier event from an earlier lifetime.

Well, I could either collapse under the weight or I could be proud of the load I carried. Although painfully hard to manage, I derived a fraction of solace from the fact that I had chosen these events to shape me for a pathway yet to come. If you have to march through Hell, at least look like you own the joint.

I guess one person's "metaphysical dick" is another person's spiritual badass...but neither one looks good on a W-2.

Real or imagined, knowing I had worked this out beforehand with other members of my soul group has helped me come to terms. And my team on the other side mitigated some of my pain. From this pain, though, came such beauty and appreciation that it lands somewhere between chrysalis and transmogrification.

The beauty of it all is that each of us are in the same boat—a boat built, in part, by our soul group— sailing on the winds of our free will with occasional navigational help from our team. Still, each of us is the captain of our own soul.

"I am the master of my fate: I am the captain of my soul."

Written in the mid-1800s by a man who had one leg amputated as a teenager and refused to let a physician amputate the other. Instead, he found a surgeon who agreed to help save his leg. Luckily, the surgeon was James Lister who is the father of antiseptic technique and where Listerine got its name. Saved his leg and made it minty fresh.

My experience set me on a course of self-exploration I would not have taken otherwise because it was going to be very challenging. But it was also a way of declaring a Control-Alt-Delete on my old life and begin a new one. In fact, I consider my coma as my "other" birthday. While everyone has a B-day, I also have a C-day.

I know I am here in refinement mode. I am also here to serve as a "spiritual paramedic." And I now recognize the spiritual themes I have been wrestling with over many lifetimes.

I am on a soul quest that has resulted in my abandonment, my murder, my suicide, and my fall from grace in the dozen lifetimes I know.

It can be depressing. It can be beautiful inspiration, too.

Why? Because this awareness now compels me, drives me, challenges me...and sharpens my focus. It dares me to divulge my most painful moments to the world in hopes that others can learn the lesson and avoid the suffering, and so they can know they are not alone. For the betterment of myself, and possibly others, I accepted the challenge. In spite of the heavy burden, I still do, or I would not have come back to this life so willingly.

But here's the plot twist. This lifetime is different.

Although my quest has been the Hydra of Hellene myth over the course of many lifetimes, I now have the tools I've never had before. Never before have I been aware of my consciousness. Never before have I had the tools at my disposal to manipulate my consciousness. How many people astral project back to a previous self, talk to that self, administer Reiki to them, and assist them during their transition back to Source?

It means that this time, when I throw a pebble into the pond, the ripples will synchronize and carry farther than ever before. I know this in my bones. I also know we all have the ability to do this.

All of us.

Listen, we may be wounded, but we are not broken! None of us is broken! Our scars are nothing more than patina. To be on Earth, at this time, means we are all spiritual badasses!

This time I am resisting the illusion of safety that conformity presents. This time I will not try to hide it or rationalize it. If I only tell the story one time and it helps only you with a struggle, then it was worth it.

As George might have said, if you're gonna fall on your ass, you might as well make a big splash.

Surf's up. Cheers!

> Mr. Mathis presented 28 days ago to the ER with Acquired Respiratory Distress Syndrome (ARDS) secondary to pneumonia. During hospitalization, he also had failure in both cardiac and renal function. Cardiac insufficiency due to separate episodes of PVCs and trigeminy which have spontaneously resolved.

It was noted that during left ventricle insufficiency a previously unknown birth defect presented itself. Mr. Mathis has a secondary AV node which took over when the primary one failed and it sustained a LV rate of 28--33 bpm. One could speculate his birth defect prevented left ventricular failure.

The cause of the renal failure is also unknown as initial response to Lasix therapy was positive. Patient subsequently gained 40 pounds which resulted in peripheral edema and third spacing even in his eyes. It did exacerbate the cardiac stress while present.

The initial cause of pneumonia remains unknown as none of the blood tests came back positive. Infectious Disease consult was also negative. Since the cause was never clearly identified, the curative component of this event also remains unknown.

Patient was extubated after 14 days. His pulmonary, cardiac and renal functions returned to normal on Day 18. Patient was discharged to step down unit.

Evaluated patient for possible physical therapy. First day out of bed in two weeks, patient walked 190 feet with one rest period. Distance confirmed with nursing. When asked how he could walk so far so quickly, patent replied "by putting one foot in front of the other."

Mr. Mathis exceeded his PT plan of care on Day 3. Discharge from hospital on Day 28.

Mr. Mathis has no idea how lucky he is.

Maybe not...but he's working on it.

CHAPTER 5

"I see your Schwartz is as big as mine." – Lord Helmet

Did you notice the dispenser in the bathroom? You can buy condoms and chewing gum from the same machine.

Seriously.

I think it's a great idea for birth control—just not how they intended.

Well, the condoms are obvious. But if you are really tanked, and you get caught trying to chew a rubber or put gum on your dick, the humiliation alone will negate any potential lustful transactions.

Seriously. Her laughter will screw with your game. Forever.

What do you mean?

Ah, it's OK for her to laugh as long as she doesn't point. Gotcha.

I think Mussolini or Napoleon said that a woman laughing is a woman conquered. I don't think he had this in mind though.

Ha! A valuable quote to deliberately forget who said it. Let's say Abe Lincoln said it.

Three cheers to Lincoln and his De-pants-i-fication Proclamation!

You're right. It's some crazy shit I'm shoveling. But I don't think this is limited to me. I just had motive and opportunity.

Yeah, I had a lot of time on my hands and no one to supervise me. I may have been grounded to my room, but I was allowed to wander in my mind...or with my mind, I guess.

So, why not you? I dunno. Why *not* you?

I've heard that difficult childhoods make for interesting adults.

No. I don't think there is a formula. Everyone has a threshold of what they are willing to tolerate. But I do think any circumstance where your physical existence is challenged can open an opportunity.

Opportunity for awakening...for satori...that state of genuine awareness when you realize your body and your consciousness have the same relationship as a race car and its driver. A car can break down during a race but that does not mean the driver will never race again. They just move on to the next car.

OK, maybe a situation where a dissociative state is created. A near-death experience would count for sure. So, too, a state created by extreme emotion, fasting, deep meditation, or pharmacodynamics.

Any Class I medication is probably capable. As well as a temporary tattoo at a Grateful Dead concert. Or a kiss from Molly while at Burning Man.

Maybe that's why some meds are under that umbrella. If people could disconnect from stressful emotions, then they'd be harder to manipulate. Lots of people before us have put engines of manipulation in place—race, class, religion, politics—to keep us miserable and malleable. For example, LDS research has shown promise in end-of-life studies as well as for those with PTSD.

What did I say?

Shit, I meant LSD. Ha!

Yeah, I don't think magic underwear is going to work. Perhaps magic mushrooms?

Seriously, though, if I believed it strongly enough, maybe magic underwear would work. Hell, I retract my snarky statement.

I also think a child is more malleable than an adult regardless of what neuroplasticity has to say. Children, like mud pies, are impressionable. Can you imagine the possibilities if we gave them the right impression to work with from the start?

Yeah…I guess my childhood was challenging. I mean, it was mine and mine alone. I didn't really compare it to others until I was in high school. By then, most of the indoctrination was complete.

I don't play that game…that my misery trumps your misery.

Well, first, it smacks of being egoic. I have met too many people who bear the standard "my pain was greater than yours," then wait for someone to pin a medal on their chest. Secondly, it diminishes the pain that the other person has shared. Part of being human is to be wounded. The other part is deciding how we will respond to it; it determines who we are.

Since we all have crosses to bear, there is no point in complaining about the splinters. I have finally gotten to a point where I don't fixate on it. But if you make a list, sure, it's long enough.

Well, I feel like I *am* here, but I am not *from* here. Death has brushed by me on several occasions but did not take my hand so my perceptions have been altered. At least that's my impression.

No, I'm not talking about the coma and the NDE. I'm not talking about the time I was held in a wooden boxcar in East Berlin by Russian police. I'm not talking about a near-miss with a midnight train in Indiana. Nor am I talking about my multiple car accidents or being shot at by a pissed-off farmer.

I am talking about my rough entry into this world that required me to stay in an incubator during the first month of my life.

Well, I was told that I was full-term, but I was just over six pounds at birth. Seems a bit underdeveloped. Maybe the parental units did not want a kid right then.

But I have another suspicion.

I have a puncture wound on my lower right abdomen that I've had since birth. Maybe it was from a coat hanger?

I was told it was from forceps. It seems incongruous, considering my small size and the fact that it is only on one side. If you grab something with salad tongs, there should be two marks.

Never mind the whys and wherefores—the sum of the pediatrician's story was this: I would always be a small and weakly child.

Go figure. I'm 6'5, 260 and got invited to the NFL Combine. So a doctor's opinion is exactly that.

What's funny to me is how Grandpa insisted on sharing his morning coffee with me. Grandma scolded him every single time saying that it would stunt my growth. All I gotta say is thank god. I'm most assuredly not a one-size-fits-all kind of guy.

That doctor may have known something about birthing babies, but he did not know this baby.

When I graduated college the first time, not only did I have two degrees, but I also had three more inches.

OK...perhaps it would be better to say that, while I was in college, I had grown another three inches.

Well, shit! Take another napkin. Sorry to make you snorkel your drink, brother.

Let me try this one more time.

It is more accurate to say that while I was in college, I grew three inches taller. So, at 6'5", 270 pounds, and in my mid-twenties, I borrowed a suit, made a dozen copies of my résumé, and went off to conquer the world, starting with a job fair in downtown Indianapolis.

Having degrees in Music and English did not exactly make me a hot commodity due to the lack of poem or song repair shops. God forbid, I was going to have to rely on my charm and guile.

Ha! You're right! I was screwed. No surprise that I ran out of résumés, enthusiasm, and time.

When I was down to my last two and with the day nearly gone, I popped into the men's bathroom to refresh, reflect, and return to the killing floor. I wanted a dry place for my folder so I set it on top of the lights above the sink; those fixtures that were probably nine and a half feet up the wall.

As I was washing my hands, another gentleman, who was also using the bathroom, came up and started washing his hands. We made the customary eye contact and head nod. He then broke Man Code by speaking to me.

He looked up, saw where I had placed the folder, and said, "Well, that's different."

I chuckled. "Well, you work with what you got."

It immediately became uncomfortable for me. The older gentleman did not exercise any discretion or subtlety; he was clearly checking me out. To add to the weirdness factor, I thought I recognized him from somewhere.

Nah. This was decades before the "wide stance" issue...nor did he have a Senator's lapel pin. It was not the time to say, "So, stranger, where do I know you from?" It was time to get my boogie on before he got his going on.

I reached up, grabbed my folder, and made a beeline out the door. Still, I knew this man from somewhere. Muttering "what the hell" under my breath, I walked out the door and nearly ran over the 1990 NFL Coach of the Year, Art Shell. You see, Indianapolis is the location for the NFL Combine.

You don't know?

For you and the 32 other people who do not know what it is, it is a place for both recruits and walk-ons to demonstrate their physical prowess in front of recruiters, trainers, coaches, and agents. By nearly running over the coach of the Oakland Raiders, I knew who had just checked me out in the men's bathroom: Dallas Cowboys coach, Jimmy Johnson.

It now made sense. I *was* being sized up in the bathroom. The next moment was damn funny. No words were spoken as I looked from Jimmy Johnson to Art Shell. Jimmy looked at me, and then looked at Art...his crooked eyebrow asking the question. Art looked at Jimmy and then at me. I've seen that look before at the state fairgrounds.

The 4H judges have that look when sizing up livestock.

"So whatcha doing here today?" asked Jimmy, with a well-practiced smile.

"I'm looking for a job at the Job Fair downstairs," I replied.

"Having any luck with that?"

"No, not really. But something will come up," I said with an upbeat tone.

Jimmy said, "Well, if you change your mind, come find me at the Combine."

He gave me a friendly slap on the shoulder and headed off with Art down the hallway.

"Work with what you got" is a good philosophy to have. So is, "Never judge a book by its cover."

Nope, I never did go down to the Combine.

Nope, I've never regretted it. I've thought about it, but never regretted it.

Because beating people down is not in my toolbox. Being a pro football player was Dad's dream. Not mine.

Jimmy wasn't wrong. Friends from my past can tell you about me going through locked doors, throwing recliners, and picking up refrigerators. But maybe it was my childhood that shaped my decision making at that point. If I was going to work 'with what I got,' I was going to have to do something else with my life.

As it just so happens, I have a decent sized toolbox. Can I interest you in some oddly shaped chewing gum? Ha!

I have enjoyed doing a great many things. I also know that I am enough of a contrarian…a cheeky monkey…that I like challenging the status quo. Challenging authority doesn't work on a football team.

Currently, I challenge authority by making a skin cream for people who are going through outpatient radiation. It addresses both the topical burn and the DNA damage that occur from the treatment. It does so by using organic and wild-crafted plants, homemade tinctures, and some Reiki.

I'm screwing the status quo because I am using what I learned while being a pharmaceutical research clinician and I am undermining a cosmetics industry that has no moral dilemma about using people as guinea pigs for profit. Screwing two industries with one product warms the 'cockle' and the cockles.

Dude, U.S. companies are pumping out chemicals with a well-documented history for screwing with people's immunity and endocrine systems. Grab a jar of a well-known cosmetic product made in both the United States and Europe and compare the ingredient lists. They're different because there are almost no restrictions on US-retailed products. I try to mitigate their malfeasance with good science, pure ingredients, indigenous practices, and Reiki.

Reiki. It's a complementary healing modality that some have equated to prayer, a laying-on of hands, and even a placebo effect.

Nope. The cream is not a medicine. It's a combination of metaphysics, philosophy, and food for your cells.

The cream is like sprinkling food in a fishbowl. It sprinkles nutrition into the extracellular fluid so your skin cells can gobble it up when needed.

It's the culmination of many things in my toolbox: nursing, plants, research, energetic modalities, nutrition, and intention. Reiki fits the bill.

Well, Reiki found me, actually.

Reiki has been a substantial part of my life for a very long time. In fact, I think it was a part of my life before I even knew it was.

In 1995, I was working in a hospital transporting patients to and from the physical therapy gym. Some of the physical therapists referred to me lovingly as "The Human Forklift." Although I spent most of my time shepherding patients, there were times when I helped them do their exercises.

During these times, I would find myself perspiring heavily. I believed this was due to the similarities of my job mimicking the "fat man" relay when I was on the high school track team. There were other peculiarities, too, but I did not make the connection.

So, when working with patients, I would zone out. Sometimes, I would see stars. Other times I would see interesting geometric patterns, colors, or fractals. The other curious thing was that my hands would get beet red and very warm. And it was my warm hands that blew my cover.

A patient I was working with had undergone a total knee replacement. I brought her down to the gym, assisted her to the mat, and began doing exercises under the supervision of the therapist. I placed one hand above her knee, and one hand on her shin to provide light resistance for her movement. She commented that my hands were really hot—not just warm, but hot.

At the same time, I noted I was sweating like a Kardashian in a confessional.

The therapist got up, walked toward me very deliberately, and put her hand on top of mine. Frankly, she was pretty hot herself...she could have touched me anywhere.

Her eyes got wide as she said, "You know Reiki!" in a conspiratorial tone.

"Who's Reiki?" was my reply. Totally a merp moment.

Turns out she was on a parallel path which started in science and led toward complementary and alternative medicine also known as CAM therapies. She offered to teach me more.

CAM therapies include acupuncture, massage, emotional freedom technique or EFT, hypnosis, aromatherapy, and so on. This therapist introduced me to Reiki, acupuncture, acupressure, aromatherapy, and music therapy all at the same time. So, Day One, after I got the horn-dog thoughts out of the way, I got my cognitive doors blown off.

At the time, I was having chronic tendinitis in my Achilles tendon.

Yes, the human forklift sometimes got injured. What I was doing was in service to others, though, so I just sucked it up. But a person can suck up only so much pain before it sticks to you like a wet fart.

Oh, come on...like you have never farted outside the car and pulled it in with you. Hell, that is one prom memory I wish I could forget.

My therapist friend clued me in to the fact that, occasionally, trauma can be carried over from previous lifetimes. I told her I don't care where it comes from, I just want it fixed. This is why I opted for several simultaneous modalities. The recurrent pain had been going on since high school, so maybe blowing the doors off was just what I needed.

The aromatherapy was already in place when I arrived at her home office; the music soon followed. There was a pallet in the middle of the floor. The aroma of Nag Champa wafted about the darkened room, illuminated only by colored candles. That, and the etheric music was at once soothing, disorienting, and relaxing.

See? That's why Mr. Mind and Mr. Happy had to negotiate for control the first few minutes after I arrived. The clothing optional statement she made also created some...conflict.

Yeah, conflict. Let's call it that. *Prost*!

Well, let me just say, I had rarely been touched in a compassionate way. Clinically? Yes. Platonically? Yes. Lustfully? Hell, yes. In that moment, I was poked in the third eye with the realization that I needed to learn the difference between passion and compassion.

Sadly, I think men in general are undereducated in that concept. I mean, most men have the emotional contrast of a Crayola eight-pack. I needed to mature; this was the first step on a lifelong journey.

Soon I was wearing my Big Dog boxers and was supine on the massage table. Any persisting thoughts about a potential 'launch sequence' ended on the launch pad. Within minutes, I had a dozen tiny needles sticking out all over my body.

I guess you could say I traded one prick for a dozen tiny pricks.

From the outside, I'm sure I looked like a human pin cushion.

On the inside, I was feeling all warm, fuzzy, and content, like a well-fed puppy with a Buddha belly. Once the needles were removed, I remained in this dream-like state. Then the therapist applied Reiki to both my Achilles tendons. And that's when the walls came tumbling down.

Because of my astral travel experiences, I was used to abstract imagery, OK?

Same thing, too, when I was in a meditative state or when I was working with patients. This sensation was similar…and different.

In my head, I was seeing movie vignettes in 30 to 60-second increments. Movies where I was the star of the show but where the physical bodies were not the one I was wearing here and now. I was the driver, but each vehicle was different.

What I realize now is that these were spontaneous life regressions bubbling up to the surface of my consciousness. Later, I would explore them in depth because of the strong emotional content that accompanied each of them.

During remote viewing and astral projection, I have always been me. I am always this meat suit…this race car. Well, that's too generous. Let's say this SUV.

The fact was, though, that each movie had me as both the main character and the director. I could alternate between the external point of view and seeing the action through the main character's eyes. One thing all of the movies had in common was that my entrance was always a pivotal moment—the crucial, decision making nexus that would trigger the close of that person's life.

Intense? HA! That's like calling an orgasm a sneeze!

That's TMI, brother. What you do with your bedside tissues is your business…unless you have a serious case of 'sniff-ilis'.

Sláinte!

Are you sure you want the answer to that?

OK, I've discovered 14 different lives, spanning from Cro-Magnon days to the London Blitz. More about that in a bit. For now, let's stay with Reiki.

After three multi-modality treatments, two things were certain. One, an energetic therapy that I did not expect to work cured me of my chronic tendinitis. So that negates the placebo effect. Two, I would get on that pony named Reiki and ride it like I stole it.

Oh, I've done some crazy cool things with Reiki. Some of which I still have problems believing.

Resetting a dislocated bone without touching it and stopping an asthma attack on someone three time zones away come to mind.

Yes…holy shit, dude.

Nope, not kidding.

Well, the asthma attack could have been a placebo effect, as the person who called me had received Reiki from me previously. But the dislocated bone? The placebo effect would have been impossible.

Why? Because it was on an animal.

Have a drink. You're losing your color.

Evidence? Sure. I used I t with my cancer patients. I looked for proof in the medication administration record. Sure enough, when I worked, my patients were using less pain and nausea medication. When I didn't, their med consumption for pain and nausea jumped to previous levels. How's that for evidence?

Like I said, have a drink.

The awesome thing is that when I suggested we put Reiki-trained nurses on the floor in 2009, people looked at me as though I was insane. By 2013, they had a pool of Reiki volunteers who could be called upon. Places like Cedars-Sinai, the Mayo Clinic, and Cancer Centers of America use energy medicine on a regular basis.

Well, just because it isn't billable doesn't mean that we shouldn't offer it.

Don't laugh. Medicare has moved Reiki to "under consideration" as a possible therapy. Trust me, once it's billable, it will get used. Patient Reported Outcomes, or PRO's, will see to that.

In my opinion, that's one thing Obamacare got right. We can't just "treat 'em and street 'em" anymore. Reimbursements now include a customer service component. Providers can no longer just provide care; providers have to act like they *do* care.

One day there will be a "famous" person who will receive a Reiki treatment induced introduction to their past self. That person will develop a "spontaneous regression," and will be cancer-free within a week or two.

You laugh…but I have been witness to two "spontaneous regressions."

Why that term? Because a "miracle" is not a billable procedure. Trust me—it's coming.

When people realize that they do not need to abdicate their own innate healing abilities to a person in a white coat, and the White Coats realize that the healing process is a synergy between two people with a common goal, we will then see fewer hospitalizations and fewer medications.

Good question. Why *aren't* we doing it now?

Because there are dozens of systems and billions of dollars being spent to keep people in the status quo. Disease is a business and you don't stay in business by eliminating your user base. You stay in business by creating and maintaining a demand.

Yes, waking up is something that should be in everyone's toolbox. And when you awaken from that decades-long slumber, wouldn't it be nice to have some signposts to help orient you to your new reality?

Here's your sign, brother.

To your health!

CHAPTER 6

"Boys! Boys! You're scaring the straights!" – Dr. Peter Venkman

Ready for another cigar? Another Mai Tai?

This one is a Kristoff Habano. It's a bit more on the robust side. You'll want to watch out for a possible head rush.

Ha! Too late for that, eh?

Can't say as I blame you.

Look, I'm surprised you haven't called the cops on me yet. I'm piling this out on you in one sitting. I usually have holy water or a holy hand grenade thrown in my direction by now.

No, I'm very impressed with you. This is the culmination of nearly 40 years of playing with my consciousness. Like the song says, I've been everywhere, man…inner space, outer space, alternative lifetimes, underground, and even the space between realities.

Scared? Honestly, yes, a few times. More than once, I thought I had gone insane or at least broke my brain. But I was definitely pushing the envelope when those scary events happened. And when you are scared, that's where you make breakthroughs. Still, because it's consciousness, it may not have happened at all; maybe I had a mini psychotic break.

Right! Maybe I ate some bread with ergot fungus. Maybe I pushed through a barrier that I—as a person, or as a human, or as an Earthling—was not expected to explore. That's one of my frustrations. I do not have definitive answers or veracious proof. But, I do ask more interesting questions!

L'chiam!

Dude, early on, I was an asshat. Before I understood anything about the concept of psychic protection, I was all over the place like a Lamar Odom hard-on. I had not read *Far Journeys* completely. Like most guys do, I read some of the instructions and then just made it up as I went along. Still, I had at least stayed in the here and now. My thoughts had not yet turned to playing with time and space...let alone dimensional realities. Still, my initial observations were damn fascinating.

My first real skidmark on the Hanes highway has to do with ghosts.

When I was 20 and projected into a haunted house I knew well and subsequently got my ass handed to me, my first of many mistakes was having a false sense of security.

It was a mansion listed on the Indiana Historic Record and is now on the National Register of Historic Places: The Wheeler-Stokely Mansion. I was the maintenance guy there on the weekdays and a docent on the weekends.

Docent...not decent. Ha! They say that dranking infects your herring. No worries. I'll let that go.

Well, at least you caught that.

A docent is a person who gives tours of a particular place and has a fair understanding of its history. I was part docent and part entertainer because I blended historical record with some of the neighborhood lore associated with the mansion.

On the contrary; I loved the place. Late 19th century Italianate architecture, wooden parquet floors, leaded glass bookcases, rich walnut paneling, centralized heating…it really was a marvel for its time. Add to that the fact it was owned by a man who became a millionaire, lost it all, and rebuilt his wealth again. In that particular respect, he was a success. But he was also an abomination.

The neighborhood lore included audacious parties that Gatsby would have appreciated, rumors of associations with the Third Reich, molestation of neighborhood children, and the suicide of the owner by deep throating a 16-gauge Sauer shotgun.

Well, like a fool tap dancing in a minefield, I projected to see what was there…or, more specifically, *who* was still there. I went. I got my ass kicked. I got the hell outta there. And I refused to project for nearly a year.

Sure, I'll take you there if you want to go.

All right, it started out as something really badass.

Why? Because I arrived at a different "when," without setting my intention to do so. I arrived at the pinnacle of the mansion's opulence. Fine rugs covered the floors…imposing leather-bound books resided behind those leaded glass doors…I mean everything was crisp and clean. Even the brass switch plates shone proudly around jet-black, push-button switches, inlaid with mother-of-pearl.

The house, in my time, was used as a music building with classrooms and offices. Gorgeous tapestries that hung where an institutional green chalkboard imposed its drabness was just one example of the sacrilege wrought by the hands of time.

Well, I think this was all part of his plan.

The ghost of the owner, William Stokely, of course.

I thought he was rewarding me for my caretaking efforts by showing me this regal beauty. What he was really doing was seducing me into dropping my guard.

Well, I chose the word "seducing" deliberately. As he was showing me around, he was directing my focus to the beauty of the environment rather than to the psychic attack he was about to unleash.

We toured the home from the attic to the basement. And I was clueless—just like the children he preyed upon—about his true intent.

One of the fascinating feats of engineering was the heating system in the house. There was a boiler in the basement for heating, but it also featured both forced air through an icehouse and a passive air-return system. It was air conditioning before there was air conditioning. I had previously marveled at the web of piping and duct work. So when he invited me down to look at it, I thought nothing of it. Once we were in the basement, the attack began.

Let me remind you that we were in his time period. I was seeing the mansion from that perspective.

The first change was when his eyes shifted from jolly to predatory. Then, his smile metamorphosed before my eyes. In an instant, it changed from warm and engaging...to the glint of a sacrificial blade.

What do you think I did? I turned to leave but discovered that he had taken control of my body. In a jerky motion, I lumbered deeper into the basement where he had a room. I had been told by teachers that was where they hung smoked meat.

You aren't kidding, oh shit!

The door opened; huddled in a corner of this iron-grey, concrete room was a small boy. He appeared to be about four years old. He was disheveled, trembling, and naked. Then, it got worse.

Stokely entered into my body.

In my head, I heard both his voice and mine. When I looked down at my hands, I saw both his hands and my hands. The final step of this possession— or infestation— was feeling his feelings. My shock at this psychic assault was his victory.

He was so very, very proud.

Why? Because this was something he'd been planning for months. And after nearly 70 years of being ignored by the living, and seeing his precious mansion stripped of its grandeur, his satisfaction with this maleficence was nearly complete.

I say nearly because of what happened next.

He/I bent over, picked up a garden hose, turned the faucet on to full, and then advanced on the little boy. It was at that moment when his plan became hideously clear; he was going to sodomize the child with the hose. And when he was satisfied, he was going to pull the nozzle lever wide open and shred the little boy's lower intestine.

He intended to reach climax and kill the child simultaneously.

It was when I began to feel myself getting an erection that I was filled with...something. The best words I have are "sacred rage."

In my mind, I screamed a thunderous, "NO!" It was so violent that there was a pressure shift in my head. Like ears popping except hundreds of times stronger and originating in the base of my skull.

It stunned us both.

Why? Because I was suddenly separated from him. A flash of insight followed instantly showing me that he meant to take possession of my soul and use my physical body to continue the horrid abominations he had committed in his physical lifetime.

What did I do? I punched him in the chest as hard as I could, spun on my heel, and ran up the stairs to get out of the basement.

Yes, he followed, all right. There was this sound—something between a shriek of rage and a thousand truck air horns going off. I believe several negative entities were hiding within the ghost of Mr. Stokely and, in that moment, they all wanted a piece of my soul.

Hellhounds on my heels. You got that right.

I slammed the door to the basement. Pausing for a second, I braced the door with my outstretched arms and splayed fingers. Again, this sacred rage arose unbidden. Through my aching head, down my arms, and through my hands, a rainbow shot through me and penetrated the door. Not onto the door; into the door. When this happened, the door merged with its frame.

There were no hinges. The doorknob had vanished as well. It was a solid wall with faux door accents affixed to it like you'd see on the set of a play.

HA! I thought I had heard trumpeting fury when I ran up the steps. But when he/they got to the door and discovered it had become an energetic wall sealing them off from the rest of the house...dude, there are no human words to describe demonic rage. If there were, I would never utter them.

When I heard that sound, I snapped back home and into my physical body with a jolt. I woke up with a startle reflex and an Elvis headache. A fat Elvis headache.

So you can see why I took a pause for a while. But, yes, I went back to it.

I initially said I'd never do it again, too. But I learned about psychic self-defense and, in a week or so, I went back to work at the same house. You can bet your ass I never went back into the basement though!

I got a cold chill every time I walked by it...but nothing happened. One day a few months later I realized that, by being afraid, I was feeding him. Or them. I had to stop doing that.

How I stopped was by remembering that feeling of sacred rage. I formed it into a neon pink bubble, and then focused on the loving feeling I had from my visitation with Grandpa many years earlier. When I walked by that door, I would imagine the bubble floating through the door.

I'm sure it pissed them off something fierce.

Nothing happened. Well, for a while.

So, I got cheeky.

I started adding an image of the little boy. I imagined him healthy, well dressed, well fed, and enveloped in the wings of a rather large guardian angel.

Yes, I'll admit it was provocative. And I did provoke something.

One evening after a party, I was locking up. As I walked by the door, I floated the bubble through it again in a very casual manner.

What happened? All four of the doorbells in the house started to ring at the same time.

Yup. Hauled ass.

You want a bite of the reality cake?

Turns out it wasn't a short in the 70-year-old wiring as I told myself later that evening. The turn-of-the-century doorbells were essentially a small xylophone with two metal bars and a hammer. Well, the doorbells had not just rung, they rang so hard that two or three layers of paint had broken free leaving paint chips on the floor.

Oh, yeah...here's the frosting for that cake: They had all been disconnected from electricity back in the 1970s.

Yup. We nurses call that a Code Brown.

I stopped the bubbles. A few weeks later, they closed down the building for renovations and transferred me to a new location.

What do I think? Maybe it was all a nasty, twisted dream inspired by something I ate or drank. But so many things have happened since, that I believe it was the real thing.

Nah, I've only smoked weed. And it was nothing like the medicinal stuff they have now; it was backyard boogie.

Then again, maybe it was true; maybe it really happened. Regardless, the important parts are the lessons and experiences that came from it.

For all I know, my guardian angels were projecting an illusion of all this to keep me from getting into real trouble. When you consider the thousands of times I've done this, having just a couple of close calls is a good record. Considering how I now blend these things together like a cosmic cocktail, I think I am doing pretty well.

OK, so none of these rabbit holes are stand-alone, even if they appear to be.

Dude, all that I have read, the lectures I've attended, the scholarly papers I've scrutinized, and my own experiences have led me to a singular conclusion: It's all connected.

Allow me to share a couple more things so you'll have more info to work with.

I'd like to talk about remote viewing which is a slightly different version of astral projection. Actually, they are adjacent rungs on the ladder of consciousness.

I think you will appreciate it because it's not solely based on experiential knowledge. With remote viewing, there is an unbiased third party who can corroborate the effectiveness of the remote viewer.

So, here we are. We're sitting here having a drink, a chat, and getting our smoke on. This is the conscious, awake Beta state. Now, imagine going home and falling into bed. Your eyelids become heavy and your breathing slows. Your brain waves will slow to an Alpha state...then even slower to a Delta state. The cycles per second are getting slower and slower. Just before you drift off, your partner or handler begins asking you questions.

Simple ones at first...How was your day? Where did you go? What did you drink?

Correct. A call-and-response action has been established. You are awake enough to hear the question. Your answers may be slow and slurred, but you're still able to answer the questions with minimal direction. That's when you make the questions more interesting, provocative, and—most importantly—provable.

How about this: Pretend I bought a new shower curtain and it's still in my trunk. What color is it? That's pretty easy in the remote viewing world as I gave you both the target and the location.

Yes, a correct reply would be somewhat impressive. But once your confidence grows, the questions can become more complex.

Well, what if I put the shower curtain in the garbage can? I then ask, "What did I buy today?" That's harder because you don't have a fixed target or location.

You have no specific target (the shower curtain); you have no location (the trash can). The twist is putting the target in an unexpected place. Who rationally buys something and then hides it in a trash can?

It messes with your head, for sure. You could be 100% perfect in the mental image you get—a packaged shower curtain in the garbage can—but disregard it because it seems irrational. Makes you second-guess yourself.

The best readings usually begin with the viewer saying, "This sounds weird, but...."

People seem able to grasp the concept of remote viewing more easily than astral projection. Maybe because it seems less "woo-woo". Maybe because it's not solely a subjective experience. Or maybe because it's been in the public awareness more than astral projection.

That may be the case until you let them know the secret of time and distance limitations.

The secret? You ready? Here goes...they don't exist.

I can remote view your kitchen today as easily as remote viewing the pyramids on Mars 100,000 years ago. Time and distance do not matter. Same things apply for both remote viewing and astral projection.

If you ask me to remote view the Pyramid of Giza, I may show up "anywhen." I could show up between 20,000 B.C. and 3,000 A.D. From the time it was under construction until its physical demise—whatever that time frame may be—that's when I could show up.

Four-dimensional thinking helps.

Imagine you are a pilot on a KC-135 refueling tanker. When you fly from Tampa to Chicago, you are flying north, a bit west, and you will be as high as maybe 30,000 feet. There are your X-, Y-, and Z- axes; your three dimensions. But you also need time: You'd be using time with velocity to get your distance.

What I'm saying is, when you are exploring a particular target, you need to know "when" as much as you need to know "where."

Let me put it this way: Looking around from the top of the Statue of Liberty in 1900 vs. in 2100, is a very different observation. Ask any remote viewer.

Yes, the government has acknowledged using remote viewers for nearly 30 years. It was called the Project Grill Flame and Project Stargate. If you've seen the movie *The Men Who Stare at Goats,* you know what I'm talking about.

So one of the tactics used during the Cold War was to outspend Russia. The U.S. utilized psychological warfare tactics to convince Russia we were creating psychic spies. The hope was that Russia would waste lots of money on this bit of psy-ops disinformation and it would lead them nowhere.

Imagine all the red, white and blue sphincters slamming shut when the Russians discovered they actually could make people into psychic spies! Suddenly, the U.S. had to play catch-up.

Yup, just like Sputnik.

Well, the Russians had their version of Project Paperclip, too. They rounded up the more esoteric scientists. Look up "Nazi" and "Antarctica" if you want to wander that rabbit hole.

The curious thing about remote viewing is that you don't get a snapshot in your head like a digital camera feed from a satellite or even the famous U2 spy plane. For example, let's say the target was the current Statue of Liberty. The handler will say they have a target. The remote viewer, with some relaxation techniques, goes to a place where the mind can be quieted.

The remote viewer will start to get mental impressions.

For example, they may say they are in a highly populated area. The handler will ask questions to help the remote viewer remain focused while not leading them. For instance, not, "Are you in the U.S.?" but, "Can you tell me what country you're in?" The remote viewer will get a mental flash or impression, something personal to them that would represent the United States. Something uniquely American.

From this point, there is a synergy—an entanglement—between the handler and the remote viewer. The remote viewer would continue by making remarks such as: I feel like I'm around New York or New Jersey. I am surrounded by water. I see tugboats going to and from an island. I see boats the color of school buses. I see many people wandering around. I get a sense of history. This is a very tall thing, but it is not a building. It's like a national icon. It is on an island unto itself.

This all sounds easy, but it takes practice from both parties. The handler must be unbiased and, to protect the integrity of the experiment, cannot ask leading questions. In my experience, it's rare for a remote viewer to respond accurately and immediately when given their very first target.

Remote viewing is not an exact science. It requires training and discipline. It is not a skill you can learn playing video games. While training, an experienced handler is an invaluable asset. They will know which impressions to hold onto mentally—e.g., things unique to the Statue of Liberty—and which ones to discard.

This is just one of many reasons why it's helpful for people to learn and practice meditation in their everyday lives. In my experience, very rarely will a remote viewer be given a target and their reply is both accurate and immediate. You have to work at it.

Once you get your bearings as a viewer, your handler can be both silent and unaware of the target. They could be handed an envelope while sitting in a room anywhere in the world. The remote viewer could then find the target person and describe the contents of the envelope.

Yes, it does sound like a parlor trick.

Well, it does have its uses.

Hypothetically speaking, let's say I view the press conference given after the crash at Roswell. I see the telegram in the hand of Major Jesse Marcel. I go to when it was received on the teletype—before it was redacted—and discover a different narrative.

Yes. Oh, shit.

Then, project to the composer. Follow him from the Pentagon to a small air base in Ohio. Follow this person until his retirement. Follow his telegraphs, his discussions, his underground meetings....

It goes on and on until you are so confused that you might as well try to play baseball on the dark side of the moon. Again, meditation helps with focus.

Some people believe that remote viewing is not, nor was it ever, a viable intelligence gathering technique. Allow me this rhetorical question then: Would different branches of the federal government fund this project for nearly 30 years if they were not getting some kind of actionable intelligence?

Another thing to consider: How many of us can afford a few thousand bucks for their own personal drone and all expenses covered to an "exotic" location?

Plus, with personal drones, the destination you seek typically has to be in the line of sight. Once you get the hang of remote viewing you can become your own handler. You set the destination wherever or whenever on the world—or off the world—you want to explore. You are now crossing over into astral projection.

You really can't have a discussion about remote viewing without talking about Project Stargate.

Project Stargate was an initiative that was financed for nearly three decades by all the important three-letter entities that exist in our government. Then, it was "shut down" in the late 1990s because the government no longer needed it. Or, one might say that the work became privatized so that it was no longer subject to Freedom of Information Act requests.

Meh. Po-TAY-to, po-TAH-to. The work continued.

In a world where things are becoming increasingly transparent, a move to make something increasingly opaque is curious, don't you think? Especially since it allegedly has no value. Right?

Interestingly, there is a group in Durham, North Carolina, which is a nexus for all these things. The Rhine Research Center.

Dude, many of the Stargate players have a connection to the Rhine. Ingo Swann, Ed Dames, Russell Targ, Joe McMoneagle...they all have a Rhine connection. To this day, they still are performing experiments related to psychic abilities, consciousness and such.

Well, they're not going to have a "Psychic Spy Clubhouse" sign, are they?

Three centuries ago this information would have been hidden in monasteries and masonic libraries. Two millennia ago, it would have been highly compartmentalized within Egyptian mystery schools. Revelation of such things would be punishable by death.

It makes the reality of Project Stargate so humorous. Knowledge that once would have had capital punishment attached to it was now part of the U.S. Army. But the Russians eagerly took the bait, began their own version of Stargate, and we all were off to the races.

I am sure there were some similarities between the two programs, but the fundamental difference was that the U.S. was using their Jedi mind tricks to learn things the U2 would later confirm.

The Russians? Well, the Russian version of Project Stargate was essentially a hit squad with a dash of Manchurian Candidate qualities. I've also heard that the Chinese have a group, the Red Hand, and they try to influence global financial systems.

Says who? Um...Russell Targ and Joe McMoneagle—former Stargate members.

It did enjoy anonymity for some time, but the cat is out of the bag now. I won't spend more time on the history, but if you're interested, I suggest you look up those individuals. Some hang their shingle out there to teach remote viewing as part of corporate espionage.

Joe is allegedly the best remote viewer of all the Stargate viewers. I was lucky to receive training from him at the Rhine Research Institute.

Professor J.B. Rhine was the Dean of Parapsychology at Duke University. When it became unpopular, the research funding shifted to donation based. You can learn psychometrics, telekinesis, remote viewing and more. What I learned there was very, very helpful.

For one, it muted my logical mind. I saw the science behind the magic. Seeing deliberate and methodical research quieted my "monkey mind," or the chatter that distracted me. My focus sharpened and the additional techniques made me more effective.

OK, here's one of my stories. I remote-viewed my lost passport.

Years ago, I had a job as an international corporate trainer teaching proprietary software to doctors and nurses. Took me to London, Paris, Barcelona...all places with both overt and occult histories.

It was November and, as I was preparing for a trip to Barcelona, I realized I had lost my passport. I searched high and low in all the typical locations. I even searched in some atypical locations. My wife at the time suggested trying to find it with remote viewing.

Calming my mind for this was very challenging. First, because I was under extreme pressure to find my passport and I did not have time to acquire another. Second, I was to stay in a place called the World Trade Center in Barcelona. This was less than a year after the 9/11 attack. It seemed a viable target.

I calmed myself into a state of light hypnosis. I imagined myself as the passport and I described my surroundings. The first thing that came through was that I felt surrounded. I was stuck in the middle of something. Squished flat. The first thing I thought was that I was stuck in between two books.

I immediately got up, went downstairs into the library, and started pulling books off the shelves. One thing you have to understand about me is that books are like puppies; I never met one that I didn't want to bring home. So, after I had pulled a few hundred books down, I remembered my lessons.

One, you never want an answer to the question of what are you looking for; as soon as you decide you know the answer of what the target is, the remote viewing process comes to a halt.

Two, your brain is conditioned to give answers—you ask your brain a question and your brain gives you an answer. Then, your brain goes back to resting anticipation. Your brain is happy with giving you an answer even if it is incorrect.

Three, build a case of evidence. If you are looking for a birthday cake, you do not want to find a birthday cake. You want to find frosting, candles, piping, a round shape, a sweet taste, an annual celebration, a check from your Grandma for twelve dollars. Tie all the evidence together. That's when you realize you zeroed in on the correct target.

Right! It takes patience and practice.

Well, I'm more patient now than what I was back then. Not by much, though.

Still no closer to finding my passport, I had to go back upstairs, lie down, and get into that head space for self-hypnosis. I projected myself back into the passport, and again, I felt the impression of being in the middle of books.

There were stacks of paper above and below me. I pushed onward to pick up other clues. The next thing that emerged was how cold I was. I acknowledged the cold. And then, what came through was darkness; it was nearly pitch black.

Yes, by refusing a solution the mind continues to give you clues.

Now, the feeling of confinement returned, except this time I felt like one of those Russian nesting dolls. Not only was I in the midst of papers above and below me, but I was confined to a very small space. Within that space was a slightly larger area of confinement, and within that space was another, even larger area of confinement.

I stopped seeking and took a moment to reassess all of the variables I had received. I asked the question, "Am I somewhere inside this house?" In my mind, I saw a pendulum swinging...and it then gave me a "Yes" and a "No" answer.

In frustration, my brain said, "Oh come on, dammit, show me something useful!" My mind showed me ladies' gloves.

Yes, ladies' gloves.

These were unusual gloves in the sense that they were old. They looked like something women would have worn back in the 40s. They were cream colored, made of silk, and would have come up to just below the elbow in a furred ruffle.

I opened my eyes and bounded down the stairs to the only place in the house, both yes and no, that was cold. To me that meant one place.

You got it: the garage.

I went out to the garage and started pawing through the warranties, newspapers, and assorted instruction manuals on the workbench. I could not find it.

Retreating into the house, I sat down at the kitchen table and ruminated over the clues I had. Somehow, I needed to add the significance of the nesting dolls, the pitch black, and the imagery of women's gloves. It suddenly became obvious.

I went back out to the garage, got into my car, opened the glove compartment, and nestled between maps and the owner's manual was my passport.

Yup, a good story. And it was good, meaningful intel that I needed to piece together. Technology does most of that for us now.

We now know that Project Carnivore scanned billions of emails a day. We know that all cell phone calls are monitored. Certain parties can tap into people's computers, computer cameras and microphones, and use drones the size of a dragonfly.

Some may think there is no need for remote viewing. But I can tell you this, it sure saved my cheese that evening.

As I mentioned, remote viewing allows you to look into places that are not terrestrial and allows you to see places in different time periods. So until we know there are time machines and spaceships from other galaxies, I think there is still a place for remote viewing.

By the way, you have three Visa cards, a Master Card, and an expired condom in your wallet.

Have a drink, brother.

CHAPTER 7

"The only good thing ever to come out of religion was the music." –
George Carlin

Oh, man, I love this song!

It's "Stairway to Heaven" by Rodrigo y Gabriela. They are amazing guitarristas from Mexico by way of Ireland.

No, it doesn't make any sense. Doesn't have to. I'm sure there is a Korean bagpipe player out there somewhere. Heck, there may even be a banjo player out there who drives a Porsche.

I've had an estranged love affair with guitars since I was eight. Football was on one side of town and guitar playing was on the other. My parents made me pick one. I chose football to please my father, but I never lost my desire to play guitar.

I'm still playing the same seven chords…but now I play them on a Martin Dreadnought so those chords sound damn fine.

Buffett and Eagles mostly. But I have some other odds and ends in my gig bag of tricks.

"Guitarristas" does not do them justice. They pluck, strum, hammer, bend, and beat their guitars into submission. And Gabriela! Dude. I appreciate a woman who plays guitar. But her? If she was gravy, I'd sop her up with a biscuit!

Oh man, I love Melissa Etheridge! She's the queen of strings! I suck like nobody's business—but if I could play a song with her, I *know* time would come to a stop. Maybe she could wear ear plugs?

She's not gay; she's awesome! OK, she's both gay *and* awesome. Her awesomeness trumps her gayness, though. I mean, I thought she was awesome before I knew she was gay.

Nah. When I found out, I was like, "OK, give her the free toaster, the L-card, and let's get back to rockin'!"

Did you see her play in 2005 when she came from breast cancer treatment to play at the ceremony for Janis Joplin? Dude—she devoured the stage! It wasn't a performance—it was a freakin' religious experience!

It was rage against the dying of the light—for damn sure.

Let me tell you...music and religion have been intertwined in my life since elementary school. I remember at Christmas and Easter how wonderful the music was, and how disappointed I was that we couldn't have music like that all year long.

Shit, I listen to Christmas music all the time. When I need to drive somewhere, I hop in the truck and listen to Christmas in the morning, pop in the afternoon, and blues after dark.

I have some religious music. Mom was Catholic. Dad was Southern Baptist. My aunt was Jewish. And I was a soloist in Catholic, Unitarian, and Evangelical churches. So I have a few songs that remind me of different performances. Since I was classically trained, I probably have a half-dozen requiems on my USB.

My voice? It's not like it used to be, but it's there when the mood strikes.

Like I said before, it was the early 70s and, in the Catholic Church, Vatican II was finding its way into music. Although I've never read it, I believe Vatican II made it obligatory to have someone in the choir who also played an acoustic guitar.

That's right. The damned hippies.

But I sure as hell wanted to be one of those guitar-playing hippies. They were awesome! At eleven years old, I thought John Denver was the epitome of cool back then. Great musician… but as it turned out, not so much of a pilot. He should have flown a little Rocky Mountain higher.

What, too soon?

Well, one of our church musicians in particular reminded me of John Denver. He played both 6- and 12-string guitars and had a smooth tenor voice that drew you in immediately. The following year when I became old enough to be a server at Mass, I had no stage fright because I had already been up there singing away.

It was during one of these holiday services that I found myself standing next to my Uncle Philip who had a strong baritone voice. I didn't know if a person could just decide to be a baritone, but I decided then and there that I was going to be one.

Of course, puberty had other ideas.

Dude, for a couple of years, my voice had more cracks than a crowded locker room.

But it encouraged me to use my ears. I wanted to be savvy like Paul McCartney—thanks, Kanye, for giving him his break—but

I also wanted the sensual tone of Lou Rawls and the insightful lyricism of Paul Simon.

It sounds righteous now, but a 13-year-old singing "You're Gonna Miss My Loving" and "50 Ways to Leave Your Lover" inspired discussions I pretended not to hear during my parent's Saturday night card games. I'm sure "special tests" were among the topics.

Actually, I've had some very interesting opportunities as a vocalist.

With a name like Johnny Mathis? Come on…

I've dabbled as much as I could as my voice coach said to never turn down an opportunity for a dogfight to perform. I've opened for the Oak Ridge Boys singing country. I performed for President Reagan singing vocal jazz. I sang a spontaneous solo in Latin while visiting Notre Dame in Paris…and my senior recital was in seven languages.

English, German, French, Italian, Latin, Russian and Japanese.

Professionally? Not in years. My coma knocked the wind out of those sails for what seemed like ages. They told me I'd never be able to sing again. Twenty some years later, German and Italian are all I remember.

But my most amazing moment as a vocalist was singing at a friend's funeral.

I was well past the "God damn God" stage and because of the coma, it essentially silenced my voice. But He knows I'm stubborn and knew I'd keep trying to sing. I also think it was God's way of encouraging me to discover another "voice"—by silencing the one I had been using. That's when I transitioned to writing in earnest… something beyond song parodies and erotic poetry.

No, no limericks. The residents of Nantucket can rest easy.

Anyway, this event was at a funeral for a good friend. Clarence "Bob" Moore had been Dad's friend since before I was a twinkle in his eye, and he came by to visit us twice a year. I thought Bob was cool because he had a hot rod—a 1951 Ford Victoria—with white leather interior and a gold paint job with metallic flecks.

He also had an interesting accent according to my Midwestern, adolescent ears. He had been born and raised on Staten Island and I was from Indianapolis. He was a tall black man; I was a short white kid. He was unlike anyone I had ever known and I liked him immediately.

Because he listened.

He was different in that he was willing to listen. Not many adults take the time to do that with small children. It is a lesson I have never forgotten. Big truths can come from small mouths. Just like big mouths speak small truths.

Bob's death was very sad.

Because he died alone. No one should die alone.

He died of a heart attack while shoveling snow and his body was not found in his driveway until two days later.

Not much was discussed the day of his funeral aside from the usual banter, but the undercurrent told me that no one wanted to linger over the fact he had died alone, frozen, and nearly forgotten.

Zion Evangelical Church was small in size but rich in history, and even when no one living spoke, its sanctuary was filled with the hushed tones of more than a century of worshipers. Finally, we got to the point in the service when the minister asked if anyone would like to come up and say a few words. To my horror, no one moved. To my left and right sat my dad and mom, lost in thought. I realize now that Dad was doing his best just to hold it together.

The minister began a slow walk back to the podium. I said not a word, but the look I gave to my mom was that someone *had* to say something. Bob was too good of a man to have silence as the final word. Mom whispered I should go up there and say something on behalf of my father or sing something on behalf of her. I rose quickly and began my determined walk from the back of the church.

I spoke about the funny things I remembered about Bob—how much he loved K-Mart, his obsession with orange sherbet, and his annual pilgrimage to the NHRA Drag Races. I also mentioned how much I appreciated Bob's willingness to listen. It seemed that, no matter what your age, Bob always had meaningful advice. The nodding heads revealed that I was not the only one who thought so.

Some people refused that wisdom just because he worked as a trash truck driver.

Wisdom comes from places you least expect... if you have the ears to hear it. That awareness would be another of his gifts that I would try to carry forward.

Then I said my mom would like me to sing a song.

I had recently learned a spiritual called "Joy, Joy." I started singing it a cappella and, rather than focusing on the words, my thoughts were drifting. I was thinking this would be the last time I could give something to him.

While wrestling with his loss, and my final gift being given, I realized someone had begun playing the organ...softly at first, and just the basic chord structure. It gave me the strength to carry on to the second verse. Somewhere during that, four women appeared in choir robes; they began to hum and "ooh" in harmony with my solo.

Sorry…just give me a second.

No, I'm good.

Brother, have you ever felt your heart break and take flight in the same moment?

I felt mine soar with this spontaneous demonstration of music, faith, loss and love. It was…transcendent. My body was singing a song and my consciousness was watching it blossom from above.

Mom told me later that every person she could see was crying—including the minister.

After the song concluded, the spell was broken. I gave a nod of appreciation to the organist and to the choir members. I very nearly made it back to my seat before I began crying inconsolably. Or—as Oprah would say—an ugly cry, snot bubble and all.

Yes, I quoted Oprah. It's OK, bro. I earned my Man Card a long time ago, and that shit is irrevocable!

To Bob…and to all good men who died quiet, anonymous deaths. *Requiem aeternam, Domine, et lux perpetua luceat ei. Requiescat in pace. Salut!*

On that day, I learned that emotional pain could be a passage to something greater than this reality. During that song, the pain, the music, and our collective intentions all gathered forces creating a sacred reality completely removed from the rest of the world.

Actually, there are myriad ways to access the divine, to transcend our humanity, and to remember our connection with the unconditional love that is God.

Music is my way and I hope you have found yours. If not, it's OK. You could spend the rest of your life looking for it and not a single day would be lived in vain. The journey is one gift; the discovery is another.

Yes, wisdom comes from places you'd least expect. A small child oft times ignored…a trash truck driver… perhaps even from some old fart tapping away on his computer keys in the middle of the night. I even found a way via a rainstorm.

Emotional pain and a rainstorm, that is.

My father died in 2000 from a massive heart attack. He stood up, probably to go get my mom, collapsed against a bookcase and fell to the floor. The TV then tottered and fell off the bookcase and onto his skull. He was 57.

Mom, a retired nurse, discovered him. She performed CPR, stopping only to get the phone and to unlock the door for the paramedics. Although the damage had already been done, she held herself responsible for not being able to continue CPR.

Ten years later, Mom had survived several more trials: her own heart attack, a crippling car crash, and cancer in both head and neck. But, when she required dialysis for her failing kidneys, she cashed in her chips and went out on her own terms.

As the Executor and only child, I had to pick up the pieces. And since she was a hoarder, there were lots of pieces to pick up. Feces and pieces, actually.

Brother, I won't even get into it. If you have seen shows on TV about hoarding, then you know what I got dealt. The most amusing thing was how she used the bathtub as a litter box. There were probably 400 pounds of litter in that tub!

It was like an archaeological dig for half of the day as I chiseled through the ammonia-soaked strata.

Well, I gutted most of the drywall in the condo from waist-level down. Redid the flooring and the bathrooms, too.

Man, I didn't know much of anything. I used to patch holes with toothpaste. But I'd watch a couple of videos online and then go do it.

It took me nearly a year, but the time finally came when I was almost done. That Florida summer had been particularly hellish. When I carried trash out to the dumpster, I could hear the grass crackling in distress when I walked on it!

One morning, I awoke in the pre-dawn hours. I was still in that Delta-wave state where one can remote view. I was relaxed…but I was also aware that I wasn't alone.

For the past several months, I had sensed my dad here and there but it was fleeting. It was almost like he was trying out a new superpower—hopping back and forth from his reality to mine.

This was different. It was a full-on visitation. I sensed him wandering around the condo and appraising all the changes I had made. Like a kid's field trip to an ice cream parlor, there wasn't a surface in that condo I had not touched.

The thing that made him chuckle was the folding doors in front of the washer and dryer. The track was always coming loose. It became known in the family as "that damned door."

The new, louvered doors glided like silk pillows falling off a bed.

So, I saw him leaning on the bedroom door frame. With a big grin he said, "You've done a hell of a job, JB."

Short for John-Boy. My dad was the only person to call me John-Boy. It was an affectation he adopted after I had become an adult in his eyes.

It was amazing. My dad was not known for being overt with his compliments. But that was just the beginning.

I was basking in my father's approval when I realized I was hearing rain. Not the harsh frog-stranglers that Florida is known for, but a steady, nurturing rain. I thought to myself, *the grass will be so happy!* And that's when I heard singing.

It was the most intensely beautiful singing I had ever heard. And I am an opera singer who has been in several cathedrals and chapels. I've even sung inside Notre Dame decades before it got torched. It was revealed to me that I was hearing Nature singing in gratitude for the rain. I was hearing the grass, the flowers, the trees, the animals...I heard them all rejoicing. I was witness to their joy for the drought-breaking rain.

I don't know how I knew—I just knew. But that music opened a mental file folder in the cabinet of my head.

It was weird. I did not know "stuff." Then it rained, I heard music, and immediately remembered "stuff." It wasn't like I had new data in my head. It was akin to instantly remembering an entire textbook from college and remembering the times and places that I had studied it.

I remembered that...that I had become music during my NDE.

Yes, I became music.

When I had my NDE.

I had neither knowledge nor remembrance of what 'being music' meant in one second...and in the next, I had full recall of becoming music during my NDE. It was weird, dude.

Seriously, it was episodes like this that made me think I had broken my brain.

So, I had just returned from the ball of crystalline fire, where I visited people, places, and things in this reality as well as other realities. My data rate was being jacked up again so that I could be directly connected to Source / George / God again.

Suddenly, I was on a grassy field that resembled a soccer field.

OK, if I'm being honest here, it was the field from the Quidditch World Cup in the Harry Potter series. The malachite field was a large expanse; its perimeter jammed with stadium seating that rose up into the clouds. Thousands upon thousands were present.

Some appeared as people—plain as you and me. Others appeared as ancient Greeks with glowing white robes. Some entities were elongated ovals of iridescent colors. And in the clouds above, angels glided effortlessly.

George spoke to the gathered assembly saying, "Everyone, this is John."

"HI JOHN!" boomed throughout the stadium.

"John is visiting us from...Earth!"

You know that "Ooooh" sound you hear when you go to a large fireworks display? Amplify that sound by infinity.

I may have already said this, but words aren't really spoken—thoughts are words and the energy of emotional content is used for emphasis. Well, in that moment, I was awash in emotional communication...and the majority of it was pure, raw admiration.

Admiration! From souls, saints, ascended masters, angels...

I was shocked to say the least.

Because I am just some farm boy from Indiana who cusses like a ball-tapped soldier, drives like a Manhattan cabbie, has fingerprints in his nose, surfs porn a few times a week, and has skid marks in his Haines highway. And they admire me!

Because from their perspective, Earth is a master's level class. Some souls adamantly refuse to go to Earth. Refuse. They'd rather study where they are for a millennium than live one lifetime on Earth. It's just too damned hard and scary.

Words are hard to come by; there is an inherent ineffability to the experience.

OK, imagine trying to perform open-heart surgery while simultaneously getting kicked in the *coglioni*.

I learned there are infinite worlds and realities in which a soul can choose to incarnate. Some worlds are purely mental. Some, purely physical. Some make both mental and physical demands but there is no duplicity.

We're a planet of liars. To each other and to ourselves. Religion, politics, marketing, relationships...

On Earth, you are wearing crisp, bleached white overalls while standing behind a sneezing cow.

Never been on a farm? OK, it's bovine excrement being projected into an oscillating propeller.

Umm...how about getting hit by a shit shotgun? Does that paint a picture?

It was so very strange. I was standing before a heavenly host in awe. That awe was magnified a thousand times over and projected back at me. Again, it was another instance of rapturous bliss.

This admiration-love-awe-respect energy wave began to flow back and forth. I felt like I was swaying…like I was floating on a raft in a pool. With each wave of this energy, my residual "humanness" was falling away. I was afloat in a sea of ecstasy.

As the layers of humanity washed away, I had an epiphany. I understood that Earth is a playground where we can exercise our free will…where one can explore the power of manifestation—albeit with a restrictor plate.

Dude! How many cars would you blow up on the highway while heading to work if you could manifest instantly? We create our own reality, but it happens in slow motion so that we don't destroy others and ourselves!

Anyway, as this mutual admiration society began to intensify, I heard singing from up above. There are no words to describe the beauty and perfection of that music. When I heard it, I felt a pull within the core of my being. It was the "Pull of Heaven"…only magnified.

I call it the Pull of Heaven because since I have been back, I have had two patients expire. During their transition I experienced vertigo, felt myself filled with that heavenly joy, and partially ascended the tunnel of light with them. This is known as a shared NDE to those who research this phenomena.

What do you think I did? I rose up to the angels and joined them in song!

At some point, their shape had changed from the stereotypical angelic forms into those elongated ovals of white with occasional pastel color shifts. Their colors rippled as though hundreds of tiny prisms were swirling in their core. They weren't just singing; they *were* music.

It was easy. I wanted to become music just like them. And then it was so.

I was no longer human. My energy signature was darker than those around me, but I was able to soar and weave just as they did…like opalescent butterflies manifesting a unique tapestry of music. There are no human words that can convey the bliss. I was a single neuron in the mind of God.

Can you give me a second, brother? I need some ice water.

When I think these thoughts too long, the Reiki furnace turns on and I don't have an extra shirt with me today.

I was once part of a Reiki share and not only did my shirt look like it had come right out of the washer, the lady sitting to my left felt the heat radiating from me. Startled her so bad that she avoided eye contact with me for the rest of the share.

There is no time over there. I was part of this heavenly energy/music until I wasn't. A cluster of energy solidified as they modulated their frequency to a lower rate. Soon, a humanoid form appeared before me. My energy rate had downshifted, too, as I was becoming a solid human form again. I was escorted back down to the Quidditch field and back to a grinning George.

I felt the urge to turn around. There stood an angel with white flowing garments, a bandolier of glowing stones criss crossing his chest, and a golden Mainz Gladius sword at his side. This was Archangel Michael.

Michael then rested his hands upon my shoulders—first his right, then his left. He then looked me in the eyes as though making some evaluation. Finally, he made the following statement with a certainty that was absolute and a clarity that was eternal...

"You...belong to us now."

Yes...wow.

My energetic self began to thicken; I became aware of my humanness again. Michael returned to the music, the Quidditch field evaporated, and I was once again in the crystalline snowflake with the silver strand connecting my energy to George. We had some parting words...and then I felt myself sinking back into this reality. The data rate slowed until I was no longer aware of it. When I opened my eyes, I was back in my hospital bed.

Yes, it is a lot to take in.

Well, years later a minister's assessment of my experience was summarized as, "I don't know what to do with you." Hell, I hadn't even include astral projecting off planet. Even then, I knew not to share that. It would have sent her reeling.

So, let me add some parting questions...just to keep you reeling.

What other mental file folders are waiting to pop open? If a rainstorm during a drought opened up the memory of becoming music, do I have more stored away somewhere?

Will there be other hazards or tragedies I must live through for these files to reveal their contents? Because it would be nice to have some share their secrets through kinder events like discovering love again.

Will this current physical iteration be able to bear those burdens or will this corporeal SUV break down? Will I have completed my tasks before then? Will the dichotomy of desires to both fulfill my quest or return home to unconditional love ever find resolution?

The fact is that I have lived many years with the thought that I don't want to be here anymore.

It's true. I have more friends and acquaintances on the other side than here in this reality. From my point of view, I have stood on the edge of Heaven. I have seen how much bliss, happiness, and rapture exist there. This place? It's a smorgasbord of shit sandwiches with an occasional chocolate truffle.

No, I know I can't check out.

I have been here for quite a while and have weathered many, many storms. To quit and go home now negates the lessons I've learned. I still have work to complete before I can go home.

But I am homesick for Heaven, brother. Every. Single. Day.

Not a day goes by that I do not remember it—not just the overall experience but the feeling of unconditional love. To be unconditionally accepted…to be admired for the victories…and respected for my tenacity to keep rising in the face of failure. It is a heavy load, for sure.

When I find myself in those dark places, I remember my OS—my Obstinate Spirituality. I remember that I have been claimed by the archangels. I remember the energetic intersections I have shared with others on their life paths and how I was an instrument to bring them back from their own darkness. It is then that I can get up off my knees and keep moving forward.

It's my contract, dude. Until I open my eyes and see my angelic escort waiting to bring me home, I shit, shower, and shave. I clothe my meat suit and see what seeds of good I can plant each day.

Yes, it is a lonely path. But it is a path I chose before coming here. At least when I project, I can taste the different realities.

I think projecting began as an escape from situations I did not like. Later, it became a novelty. Then, it became a quest to see how far I could push my boundaries. At some point, I ventured past the point of "normal" reason and common sense.

HA! Good one! I can't share this shit with just anyone. My online dating profile might get a look every month or two, but I've had people block me after I take just one peek at their profile.

Don't get me wrong. There's good stuff in this life, too. I have helped to bring a handful of medications to market and have eased the suffering of thousands. I have sung songs and written words that have moved people to action or lifted them up so that they could take a pause in the comic opera of their own lives. As a nurse, I have comforted both minds and bodies as they both came and left.

I guess I'm saying it's a lonely life, but I believe it is also a necessary one.

There's a saying: "I have drank from wells I did not dig. I have been warmed by fires I did not build." That means there was at least one person who was thirsty and cold but who ignored their own discomfort and created an oasis for the benefit of others.

I believe I belong to both groups. We all will eventuality.

Why, yes...we are way past our favorite guitar players.

CHAPTER 8

We're all vehicles in the service of angels or demons depending on how much coffee we've had.

Is it dark in here or is it just my personality?

So, do you understand now why I think painful things like turning off my parents' life support, however tragic, were both normal and grounding? How things like divorce and bankruptcy kept me grounded in this reality?

Right. After flying around Heaven and hearing plants singing in gratitude for rain, dealing with family issues—however repugnant or painful—reconnected me to this reality.

Yes, on one hand, it is all an illusion. The life we are living here on Earth *is* an illusion. I'll borrow from the Bard—Life is a butt stage and we are merely butt players. The end.

HA! Yes, please. "Ass me a question."

But so is going to a movie. It is an illusion where we all agree to willingly suspend our reality and belief systems so that we can enjoy the ride. And what's the definition of a good movie? It is getting lost in the narrative. It is a temporary suspension of your story while observing another's. For two hours you are in another reality eating ten-dollar popcorn and drinking five-dollar sodas...unless you are like me and sneak in a six pack. Life is the same thing. Just as we have no qualms about handing over two hours of our lives for a movie, what is the big deal about handing over 80 years of your life when you are eternal?

OK... Some movies are harder than others to get into, but others are special. They suck you in; you become emotionally invested. You align yourself with one of the characters. And when it's over, you have to sit a few minutes in the theater and let the mental milieu steep and settle. That, brother, is life.

At some point, I finally realized that I am the main character of my story as well as the director. Not only do I act and react to my story, but I can also choose how to act and react to things. Those choices shape the narrative.

Bingo! Thoughts become actions; actions shape events...and this is how we spend our universal currency known as free will.

True. Some actors get lost in their roles. Another part of yourself has to bring the actor in you back to reality.

I think I'm like any number of other people who are drawn to those in need...to give them cues that help them get on with their individual stories. But I don't think such helpfulness is imparted only by people who feel that call. We have all intersected with and affected the lives of others. No man—or woman—is an island.

For example, I am remembering a time when I crossed paths with a minister. I was dressed as a nurse, but I ended up being a Sherpa. I just didn't smell like yak sweat.

It was when I was working the night shift on the oncology floor. His wife happened to be my patient.

Being an oncology nurse is like being in the Peace Corps, my friend. It's the toughest job you'll ever love. At least, that's how I felt about it while my marriage was falling apart and I was squatting in a coworker's spare room.

Because no matter what chaos, instability, or anger I felt in my own circumstances, it paled in comparison to the trials and tribulations surrounding me from 7:00 p.m. to 7:00 a.m., three nights a week.

Brother, I was surrounded by such bravery, determination, and—in some cases—surrender, that it humbled me. If not for my coma a few years before, I would not have seen it this way. To share in their movie...their sacred space...was a privilege and an honor that I shall remember always.

You sure you want to hear this?

OK, let's reload. How about I get us both a real Mai Tai?

Dude! You can't drink at a Tiki bar and not have a real Mai Tai.

No, no, no, no...there is no OJ or pineapple in an authentic Mai Tai...only lime. You need to follow the traditional Trader Vic recipe as much as you can. Sadly, the original 17-year-old Wray and Nephew rum is selling for $55,000 per liter, so you have to pivot from that to J. Wray or the Appleton Estate rum. If worse comes to worse, you want a 17-year-old Jamaican rum that has a dash of molasses in it.

Let me order. If you don't like it, I will drink yours for you.

Hello, gar·çon. I would like to order a Mai Tai as close to the Trader Vic's recipe as possible. Do you have any 17-year-old Jamaican rum that has been blended with molasses?

Good! Do you have fresh lime juice?

Great. How about both orange curaçao and orgeat?

Orgeat—it's orange flour water and almond. If not, almond syrup will do.

Do you have simple syrup made from unrefined sugar? Excellent!

So here's what I need:

> 2 ounces Appleton Estate Reserve blended rum...Denizen Merchant's Reserve if you have it.
>
> 1 ounce of Wray & Nephew White Overproof rum
>
> ¾ ounce of fresh lime juice
>
> ½ ounce orange curaçao
>
> ¼ ounce of orgeat...almond syrup if you don't have orgeat
>
> ¼ ounce of rich simple syrup

OK, now you need to shake it with 12 ounces of both crushed and cubed ice and make it frosty. Pour ice and all into a double old-fashioned glass.

No, no umbrella. Tradition says to top with a mint sprig to mimic a palm tree and a half lime to mimic an island.

Now, this is a Mai Tai as close to the Trader Vic version until all the traditional rum was gone. When it migrated to Hawaii in the mid-1950's, it got adulterate with orange juice and pineapple because...well, it's Hawaii. Later, Bacardi came along and homogenized rum production and the original was nearly lost to history.

Let me know how history tastes?

Excellent. Now, let us forge ahead.

So, I will tell you a story. It's a love story…but not like the ones you're familiar with. It is also quite sacred to me personally, so thank you for indulging me.

It was time for my midnight nursing rounds and I made my preparations for entering into my patients' rooms. Having been a patient myself for almost a month, I was acutely aware that sleep is a precious commodity in a hospital. My Six Sigma mentor taught me this mantra: Be Brief, Be Brilliant, Be Gone. So with as much ninja skills as my NFL lineman frame would permit, I slid stealthily into my patient's room.

It was a dark chamber back lit only by the sodium lights from the parking lot a few stories below. As my eyes adjusted, I noticed a man sitting at the foot of his wife's bed. Well into her eighties, the cancer had distilled this lovely woman into ninety pounds of faith, determination and pain. I was here to address the latter. In return, I would be given a dose of the former.

My eyes continued to acclimate to the surrounding coral-tinted dimness. I could make out her husband much better now. His sweater and dress shirt reflected the distress he had been increasingly under since beginning his vigil a few days earlier. His shock-white hair was in disarray as much as his life appeared to be. Simultaneously, it became evident that he was massaging her feet and softly singing church hymns to her.

Brother, let me tell you, I froze in my tracks.

Because I did not want to intrude into this sacred space.

First, this was one of the purest demonstrations of love and devotion I had ever witnessed. This man, a minister, was sharing a moment of true love with his partner of over 70 years. And although there must have been thousands of similar moments before this night, there remained but a few of these sacred moments between them going forward. I would not deny them that.

You say beautiful—but it was more of a bittersweet moment. Still, it most certainly was sacred.

The other thought I had was my own unworthiness. I did not deserve to be there.

Seriously, dude. The slow-motion train wreck of my own marriage surely had left some stain upon me. I wanted to protect them from that horror; I did not want to corrupt them with my misfortune.

You have a point. Maybe I was becoming conditioned to observing happiness rather than expecting the experience of it in my own life.

Anyway, whether she heard my entry or felt my discomfort, my patient opened her eyes and gave me the biggest smile. She invited me in to perform my duties. Respectfully, I declined and said I could come back, as I had other patients I needed to see. She told me not to be silly, in such a disarming way that I smiled and stepped forward to complete my tasks.

I made pleasant small talk as I worked, all the while ruminating over the depth of soul-connected intimacy that lingered and encompassed them. In the darkened silence, it was radiant and permeating. To this day, I still believe I was blessed to be in their presence.

So I thanked them for their time, apologized for the intrusion, and made a beeline for the door.

"I hear you used to sing a little bit," she said.

I don't know how she knew. I replied that I had sung many years ago, but had returned to school to become a nurse.

Dude, at that point in my life, the world seemed to have more people who were sick than who appreciated opera. With a mortgage, a family, and a couple of student loans, it seemed the prudent thing to do. Later, I would realize I had traded one opera for another.

"I'd really like to hear you sing," she persisted.

My nursing experience to that point had been limited, but my credo was this: If it was in my power to give, I gave. An extra ice cream, a pillow from an empty room, a back rub with a warm washcloth…all of these things made me feel like a person when I was hospitalized. I never forgot those kindnesses, and I made damn sure to pay it forward whenever I could.

So with that mindset, I sang a very prayerful version of "How Great Thou Art" for them. This song has meaning for me as I had sung it at my father's funeral a few years earlier. It had been his favorite. In fact, I still sing it to him when I'm driving.

They both complimented me and told me I should keep singing. I told them I had been doing it the better part of 30 years and that when the time was right, I would do so again. So with a smile and a wave I headed once more toward the door.

"John, do you think God will let us keep her until Christmas?"

I froze again. Singing a hymn in a darkened room is one thing; assisting a minister during his dark night of the soul is quite another. I felt so underqualified in that moment.

"Well, her labs indicate that she's holding her own for now, but I feel that her oncologist would be better suited to answer that question," I replied.

Even as the words fell from my mouth, I could see his expression glaze over as though he had heard this medical-speak before, so I continued without a pause.

"But you are asking me to peer into the mind of the Creator…to know His will…and to be able to offer you some solace."

His gaze cleared immediately so I continued.

"I also know that, as a minister, you have had many people over many years come to you and ask you the same question. I am not a minister and I feel any answer I can give you would be pure speculation. What I can truthfully tell you is that the love I see between the two of you is one of the most beautiful things I have ever seen."

Yes, I actually said that.

I told them, too—though I may be paraphrasing a bit—to see such love, to feel such warmth, is surely a sign of God's love and of how it continues to manifest between the two of you. There are people who will live their entire lives never experiencing the kind of love you have for one another. I believe God grants us only so much time in this playground before we must return home…and as long as we have lessons to teach or learn, then we know our time is not yet finished. You both have taught me a lesson here tonight and I feel that your love has other lessons to teach. So…I think you both will be here for some time.

I could see the glistening streaks on his cheeks in the muted light. He managed to ask another question as he strained for composure.

"She's been with me for so many years. I just don't know what to do. Do we need to do more chemo? Do we need to do more surgery?"

I pulled up a small stool and sat down next to him. I put my hand upon his and offered him a suggestion.

"Before you were a minister, you were a husband. And I can tell that you are a steadfastly devoted and selflessly loving husband with ferocious determination. You have fought admirably for her and have labored hard for her to live with dignity."

It was here when I noticed his bottom lip began to tremble. For me, it was hard to process...to see someone bearing the burden of so much love and so much pain within the same moment. He was both tightly wound and unraveling before my eyes.

I concluded, "At some point though, you will have to fight just as hard for her to leave with dignity. I don't know if that will be before or after Christmas...but I do know this. When that time comes, you will have sorrow...but you will also have no regrets."

Here, take this napkin, bro.

The minister slid his arm around my neck and gave me a hug which I returned. I felt his warm tears running down my neck. I imagined a Reiki symbol in my mind to promote his healing. I then became aware of his wife as I felt her hand on my other arm.

Brother, it wasn't amazing—it was transcendent! This synergistic moment of love among three injured souls was healing for us all. Amidst the tears and sniffles from everyone finally came laughter and more hugs.

There was a healing in that hospital room that night...and it had damn little to do with the medication I had brought with me. I left the room an unmistakably different person than when I went in. I learned that no matter the illness, state of mind, or station in life, we all have access to the divine. We only need to take the time from the comic opera of our lives and invite it into our hearts.

That is one of life's secrets: The connection to Source is always there. The sun is always shining...even in the darkest night.

So what happened? By my next shift, my loving couple had left and returned to their home. Such is the life of a nurse. I silently wished them well and moved on as another patient had occupied the room; the health care cycle would begin again. The final outcome would remain a mystery...or so I thought.

Time passed and I accepted another job. As my exit interview drew to a close, my manager stated that this hospital floor was unlike most in that there was usually some event that left an imprint. She asked me for mine. I had several, but I told her the story of me singing to that couple and the remarkable love that each demonstrated for the other. She popped out of her chair as if something had bit her on her perfectly proportioned ass! I sat in stunned silence as she went to her filing cabinet, pulled out a hand-written letter, and handed it to me.

"This belongs to you."

Quirking a curious brow, I read.

> *To whom it may concern,*
>
> *Thank you for taking care of my mother during her short stay here. You treated her with such grace and dignity. I especially want to thank the male nurse who sang to my parents. Your song in the night and the time you spent were a blessing and brought her such peace. My father and mother had known each other since grade school and had never been apart.*
>
> *We prayed, as did many others, that she would stay with us through Christmas. Please know what a difference he made in their lives. They both spoke lovingly of him at our Christmas service. Please let him know she made it through Christmas; Mom died mid-January surrounded by family singing church songs to her.*
>
> *You were a blessing. Thank you.*

And I never got to say "thank you"— for they showed me that unconditional love can exist on this earthly plane.

With no trace of hyperbole, I can say that, in my heart and mind, this memory will be forever cradled. And cherished beyond measure.

Here, have another napkin.

CHAPTER 9

I want to live in a world where sin-eaters need food stamps.

You know, there are some mysteries that should remain just that—mysteries.

No, I'm not even talking about the near-death thingy. I'm talking about hot dogs.

Don't laugh, dude! I mean, seriously, I would like to have been there for the very first taste test.

"Hey buddy, you like pork? Here, try this small sausage I created—something for the person on the go. You just boil 'em up and eat 'em."

"Here, have a bite. You like? Excellent!"

"I think that, with a bit of mustard, people would eat them by the dozens."

"What do I call them? Snout…lips…and taint surprise."

Dude! It's dog food in a shit chute! Ground up taint in a wrapper made from washed intestines. Who the hell thought that would be a good idea?

Seriously, I don't know who deserves the pimp-slap: the creator of such an abomination or their marketing department.

Same thing as scrapple. Makes my stomach churn.

Yeah sure, haggis is right up there. Just like that Swedish fermented fish...*surströmming*.

Well, when Thor's hammer is in my head, my go-to bender food is a slider. You know, a White Castle burger.

Yup, kinda like a Krystal burger but steamed. And without mustard as part of the standard issue. What's your rescue food?

A gyro? Really? I never heard that one before.

Everyone has a different survival plan, I guess.

So, where do you want to go now? Forward? Or circle back?

OK, circling back to PLR—past life regression. I knew you were gonna say that.

Sorry. Bad psychic joke.

How did I find them? Accidentally...if you believe in accidents. Otherwise, I'd say it was a corked bottle that popped open in my head when my head was ready for it.

The question I am still working out is who decided it was a cork and not a bank vault door? And who decided on what the criteria was for me being ready?

My first PLR episode was during one of my very first Reiki treatments. I was getting Reiki, acupuncture, and sound therapy all at the same time for chronic Achilles tendinitis.

Yes, the hot therapist.

Overall, the experience was like opening the windows of a musty house during a refreshing summer rainstorm.

Well, as I said, I was in a light sleep—or a similar hypnotic state. I was still aware of the music and occasionally responding to my therapist as she adjusted the needles.

Nah, no pain; just the pressure of it being tapped in. There was a tingling sensation as she perfected the placement. Like many things, it was weird at first and then it's a positive experience. Afterward, you feel amazing.

At one point, she asked me how I felt. With slurred speech, I replied, "Floaty." She laughed and said she'd let me be.

I was just over 30 years old, so I'd already been astral projecting for nearly 15 years...and I had the familiar feeling of disassociation. I saw Reiki symbols, sparkles, and sacred geometry floating in the ether of my mind. Very soothing.

Suddenly, as though someone had changed the channel on the TV, the picture changed. I was standing in a tipi. There was only a fraction of a second of disorientation before full immersion.

Yes, kind of like in *The Matrix* when Morpheus gives Neo the martial arts lesson.

What was I doing? I was saying goodbye to my wife.

Because I was going off to die and we both knew that my death was nearly certain. The other certainty was that I had to go with the group as our leader had declared we must.

It was a dichotomous perspective, again, because I had both an external and internal point of view. I was seeing through both the actor's and the director's eyes. Or, you could say I was seeing it from both body and soul perspective.

I could see us standing chest to chest; our rhythmic breathing synchronized so that with each exhale, we drew closer together. I also knew our eyes were closed. I focused on her breath upon my neck. I felt our foreheads touching and our fingers interlocked as though we were passing energy back and forth.

The emotional energy was overwhelmingly intense…more prominent than any other sensory perception. Between us circulated unconditional love. It moved both in us and through us.

It was the pinnacle of intimacy.

That was the first time, in this current lifetime, that I experienced unconditional love—and it was an emotional overload. I began gasping as though tasting oxygen for the first time.

My practitioner friend had not strayed and, in a soothing tone, she navigated me through the experience.

First, she asked me whether this was a dream or something else. It was most assuredly something else. She then asked me to look at my body and describe it. When she learned that I was seeing it from both a personalized and depersonalized point of view, she kept me in that later state to help with the emotional waves.

Dude, it was incredibly strong! Because I had been abused throughout most of my childhood, all I knew until that moment was conditional love. As a child, any overt signs of love were my reward if I got good grades, did my chores, did as I was told, and didn't misbehave by being too loud or boisterous. When you grow up in chains you don't know any difference. When they are removed, you are shocked on several levels.

Like my later NDE, I went, in an instant, from a state of not knowing to a state of knowing. The history, the crisis, what role I was there to play, who my wife and children were...the whole enchilada.

The situation was a crisis within a crisis, and it stemmed from our chief's ego. It was why we had splintered off from the tribe as a whole.

I told my friend that I belonged to a fragment of the tribe. We left because our chief was planning a war which many felt was unnecessary. With shamanic insight, I saw a horrific outcome fraught with bloodshed and lingering sadness. So, several of us left.

In the tribe, I was the holy man—a medicine man with the gift of visions. What I had failed to see was that the coming bloodshed was our own doing and not the result of the impending war our chief was planning.

Not many. There were fewer than 25 of us; we were conscientious objectors. We were avoiding a war with another tribe. The chief's motivation wasn't survival or even resources. It was his pride.

With lower numbers, we thought the chief would reconsider his war plans.

The exact opposite happened.

Conflict within our own faction grew when we left as it dishonored the chief. We were ordered to rejoin the tribe and fight...or be killed. Some thought it was better to call his bluff because it would shock him back to his senses. Some thought it better to die at the hands of our brothers than to wage war on strangers who bore us no ill will. After much discussion, we decided to return.

That morning, as we were riding back to the tribe, I experienced another flash of precognition and it held the knowledge that we were riding to our deaths. There was no way to prevent the war. It would solidify the chief's authority, feed his ego, and it was the only way the chief could save face.

When the war party left, two others and I rode our horses backward so that we would not be disconnected from our loves. The emotions of leaving unconditional love to attack a tribe we had never officially met, and to protect the pride of an egomaniac was gut-wrenching—pure and simple.

As I watched my wife's form grow smaller and smaller in the distance, I felt the bond of love grow stronger and stronger. It pushed out almost all other emotions.

The flame of my anger was small but would not be quenched. I struggled to maintain my composure while attempting to focus on our time together and the blessings I had shared with her...when the channel changed again.

Yup, it was that quick. Again, like changing channels on a TV.

Now, I was standing on the deck of a ship. If you know something of ships, it would appear to be the cousin of the infamous brigantine called the Mary Celeste. It was a two-masted merchant vessel and we were at war with the elements.

How did I know? Because the night was black as pitch save for the frothing waves crashing over the bow. Angry rain stung my face and neck. My crew's mounting fears were heightened by the occasional blast of lightning giving us intermittent and terrifying glimpses of waves that should have swallowed us whole.

Death was upon us, pure and simple.

The rigging was in disarray; the slap of wet material told me that the sails above, which had not been properly secured, were becoming hopelessly shredded in the bitter wind. Occasionally, I would be lashed by an angry line made heavy with seawater. Through it all, I could still make out cries from below to loved ones, to mothers, and to God—none of whom were available to help us. Personally, I had no love to call upon but that of the sea...and she was all teeth and no ears.

My ship was undersized compared to others in the East India Trading Company, but she was quick and had a shallow draft. The fact that we had never been pirated, never lost our supplies, and never lost a man, was a point of pride with me as her captain. It also pleased our investors and enabled us to contract our services for higher amounts.

Well, our perfect record was about to come to an end.

This ship, as good as she was, had no rightful place in the open ocean. She was meant to be fast, quiet, and violent if the need arose. I knew I was taking a risk by sailing so far from shore, but I also knew it was a tactic that pirates would not anticipate. I was known among my men to be cunning, brave, and lucky.

Good catch! Yes, the previous lifetime was dying because of someone's ego. This death would be brought about by my own ego. It's a variation of a theme I would repeat in other lives.

The periodic images revealed by the lightning illuminated a slow-motion catastrophe in the making. The load on the deck was shifting because of the relentless waves; the ship was listing to starboard, and the hold was filling with water.

The weight of my guilt made it even harder to breathe. I resolved that my ego was not going to kill my crew without me fighting for their lives. So, against all rational thinking, I untied myself from the wheel and tied it in place.

I staggered across the midnight deck toward the netting and crawled up the high side. Pulling line from wherever I could, I tied off crates at the top and then shoved them over the high side so that they would counterbalance the rakish tilt of the ship.

I knew wet ropes would be stronger. They would hold the crates until the storm abated. My cock-sure bluster began to billow again.

As I was crawling back to the wheel, one of the crates came loose, caromed off another crate and crushed my left leg just above the ankle...nearly amputating it.

I roared! Not in pain, but in rage!

Rage that my luck had run out and that my ego had got the best of me.

Rage at the fact that I would forever be less than a whole man.

Rage that I would be one of those pathetic peg-legged ghosts that haunted the docks and taverns...telling stories of the past while the rest of the world looked to the future.

Rage at knowing I was now part of the flotsam of history.

Knowing my life and career were over, I cared not for my body. I pulled my dagger and vented my rage upon what was left of my leg. I laughed maniacally at the irony of freeing myself from one prison only to trade it for another.

In a near-psychotic state, I crawled to the wheel, tied off my leg, and wrenched the wheel to correct for the list and the subsiding waves. Then, I began to feel numb.

I vaguely remember lying on the deck, drenched from head to single foot, and feeling nothing. From my handicapped view of the world, the storm raged in my right ear while the moans of the tortured ship reverberated in my left. Both were muted by the rage in my head.

As different crew members stumbled to my aid, I thanked God for the rain so that the men could not see my tears. I was a dead man and they were too drunk on the idea of cheating death to see it.

Once home, I was declared a hero. A goddamned hero.

Ho! Celebrations would continue for a week. I had risked my life for the gallant crew, the ship, and her cargo. For that week, no man was my equal. But I had paid dearly for my fame. My perfect record would stand…but I had paid for it in blood, tears, and substantially more than a pound of flesh.

The next time I set sail, I knew it would be my last. My love for the sea was gone. I was no longer part of the ship.

It was a fraction, a shadow of a man, who then stood upon her deck. And, while the countenance of some men reflected awe and admiration, in others I saw the poison of sympathy. It served only to stoke my already white-hot rage.

The ship's perfect record continued. The trip was without incident…and without joy. As dusk embraced the harbor, I was the last to leave the ship.

I took a solitary bag, holding all the worldly possessions accumulated in nearly 30 years at sea, and resolved never again to set eyes upon a ship or the sea. I clumped my way to a ratty inn, rented a room—which I privately called my mausoleum—and drank myself to death within a week.

On my last day, I remember throwing the brass sextant into the room's stove and watching the firelight dance in the scale-magnifier glass. I thought to myself that it would not serve me on the journey I was determined to take. From there, my memory goes black.

Yes…damn.

Not many people have the experience of seeing their way of life—their identity—stripped from them in a moment. That cursed spectacle is usually insidious.

Yes, it's true. Those who survive a natural disaster—like a hurricane or an election—can lose their belongings, family, and a livelihood that took decades to build and it can vanish in an instant. But there is a gift in shared bereavement. There is support from extended family who are not affected.

But this man had possessed none of those things. He had run away from an uncaring family when he was 12. He had been welcomed onto his first ship because of his strong back and keen mind. He had reveled in having the sea as his true companion...and now...even she had grown weary of him.

Some people have learned that after a wound's physical healing, or a profound change, comes the awareness of the wretched term "a new normal." Some people have the fortitude to pivot and embrace the challenges of that altered state. Others do not and take their own lives. And the truly broken sometimes take innocent people with them. God knows we have seen enough of that in the news.

This person, the captain, had pivoted on several occasions as life was not kind to him...and I know some religions are quick to condemn suicide. But until you have been forced to pivot several times...to be broken at a fundamental level...you cannot not understand. Surrendering a part of your identity—or having it violently ripped from you—is the only way to truly know. Until you have surrendered your identity for another—one for which you cannot seem to get your bearings—you cannot possibly fathom the agony.

Brother, when you have pivoted several times in your life, the ultimate surrender may be the only solution. You can only fold your cards so many times before you have to step away from the table.

So, when I awoke back in this reality, my face was wet with tears as the burden of previous lives settled into this current one. Being one person, and now having three sets of memories, was nearly paralyzing in the moment...and would be the cause of many meditative sessions to follow. Also, the process of accommodation can nearly drive you mad.

You're right, maybe I am. But I did create a resolution to the original crisis.

My resolution? My ankle never hurt like that again. But I had traded physical pain for existential pain...like trading a paper cut for a hemorrhoid.

At first, I was shocked that I had known such shitty lives. I realized that I had not been at the cosmic Costco sampling all the products. Instead, I had chosen the abandonment aisle and had put every damned item from the shelf into my cart!

I felt better though. Within a couple of days, I realized that I am a hell of a lot stronger than I give myself credit for.

After all was said and done, I had received more than a healing.

Physically, I obtained a permanent resolution to the chronic ankle pain that had vexed me for more than twenty years. But that was trivial compared to the expanded consciousness I received.

Wow, indeed. You do have a talent for understatement, sir.

Yes, I went back for more.

Why? Because a stretched mind cannot return to its original shape.

In my mind, I exchanged one pain for several others. But, in the exchange, I also grew. The expanded consciousness... the awareness of past lives... the universal lessons that united all the lifetimes... it was knowledge with pain. It was wisdom.

It hurt to say yes, but I could not say no. And now I can say "know" with a capital 'K.'

Yes, there were other lives with similar stories, but the captain's story is the life I chose to explore in depth.

No, I didn't bother to research who he was. The message is the important thing here...not the messenger. I do not require proof of reincarnation.

What I mean is that the emotional connection and context is more important to me than the historical figure. I'm more interested in my soul's family tree than my genetic one.

I am also aware of having been a schoolteacher in the Old West. He, too, was isolated. His intelligence was threatening to most, so most people avoided him. He had so much to give, but his methodology was off-putting. So he had all this knowledge to share, but he did not have the wisdom to parse it in a nonthreatening way. His anger and frustration at his blunted utility led to his death by heart attack. He died in his schoolhouse...full of books and empty of students. It feels too close to this lifetime for comfort's sake.

Once, I was a warrior in feudal Japan. Again, a bad childhood. This one resulted in a desire to punish. I rather enjoyed killing. I remember studying anatomy and physiology so that I would become more efficient in my killing. I remember being shocked at how fragile, and yet simultaneously resilient, the human body was.

What should have killed instantly did not always do so. I realized we're more than meat. In this satori, I dedicated my life to restoring my honor and living a life of contrition.

Why not penitence? Because contrition has an undercurrent of finding absolution. Then again, that may be due to my Catholic upbringing. One can be humble in their endeavors but not have any expectation of absolution...or at least discovering some peace of mind. Contrition is a state of mind which is present when you are performing the same endeavors, but the expectation is that you will eventually balance the karmic scales of justice. At some point, spiritual restoration is achieved.

In this lifetime, I have a distinct memory of kanji writing on thin strips of bamboo with a brush made from my own hair. I do not speak Japanese, but I remember the last image having three upstrokes that looked like swords. I had a sense of irony as I thought they represented my past...the lowest stroke...my present, and my future...the highest stroke. There was also a phoenix mythology wrapped into this emotion, but I could not get any more specific than that. As I was writing, I heard a voice saying something like Akuna-o-kahgee...Kahmi-o-kahgee. He just kept repeating it over and over.

No idea. It confused the shit out of the online translator. It offered up suggestions in Finnish and Swahili. But when I meditated upon it, the mental picture I got was the Yin-Yang symbol made out of a big powderpuff looking flower. It was very dense with small delicate petals. It was about the size of a baseball and was cream colored with a subtle shade of purple. I was remote viewing the memory of a former self so I can't verify anything. I asked for more information, but I was shown a blank chalkboard which is my symbol for no more information.

That image was at the end of his life. As a young man, he would later adopt something similar to the Bushido Code but with an esoteric vibe. He went into the mountains where there was less distraction and created his own school. The students would become herbalist healers before even picking up a weapon. They would be called Yamahoshido. Think of them as part Merlin, part Sherpa, and part Templar Knights.

I don't know if it's real. I own a Yamaha 1700. Maybe my brain cobbled together the word?

In another lifetime, as a member of the Knights Hospitaller, I would again be a warrior-healer and explore that dichotomy. This lifetime was rather piquant as I remember being in battle with my twin brother. He was possessed by the same bloodlust that I had selected in the previous Yamahoshido life time while I was more focused this time on the esoteric healing of this sect. Twin brothers, but he was the Yang to my Yin.

I remember us both standing on a hillside following a particularly egregious battle. We stood shoulder-to-shoulder— weary, bloodied, and grateful. I noted the black crusaders' cross on my tunic and the red one on his. I then looked upon his face and realized that this brother was also my father in this current lifetime. It's interesting to note that, in this lifetime, we shared the same birthday—just 24 years apart.

So, in another life, I was a Cro-Magnon male exploring an unfamiliar area where the grazing was plentiful and the flowers were more than pretty to look at. They psychically beckoned me to use them for different ailments. They were my tiny, eager assistants ready to help. While gathering them, I was surrounded and captured by another group of early humans who had smaller frames. They looked like hobbits on steroids. They were territorial, and my size scared them, so they tied me to a tree and used me as target practice with wooden spears. My last memory was the adults turning over the weapons to the children to use for practice.

I was also a mother during the London Blitzkrieg. While running with my infant daughter, I would see my husband and son die in an explosion directly in front of me. The only other memory I have of her is breastfeeding other infants whose mothers had died in exchange for food.

I was a Nubian slave in Egypt whose physical prowess was unmatched until a jealous slave broke my ankle. Unable to work, I was starved to death. For some reason, he did not have the power of speech.

I was an undefeated Sumo wrestler whose vices and decadence ruined his reputation and his life.

I was a Vatican cardinal who would not take a mistress. The mounting distrust among the other cardinals resulted in my assassination.

There are a couple more, but I have never cultivated a relationship with them beyond a snapshot.

No, never anyone famous. Just a meat suit working through the lessons I had set up for myself before diving into the next gene pool.

There were a few that did not end tragically, but most did.

My current understanding is this: Anytime you gain knowledge without pain...humans lack the appreciation and depth of the wisdom that accompanies it. In my mind, it is a way of making sure that a soul's reach does not exceed its grasp. Once I recognized that there was no longer a need to look backwards, I stopped. A rear-view mirror is nice, but you don't want to make it a primary focal point...although there are a few Florida drivers who may not have learned that particular fact.

Hell, I've seen a driver rolling down the interstate with their seat belt outside the car and kicking up sparks of the road. I saw another rolling down the highway and his speedboat and trailer were only attached by the safety chains. The hitch was also tossing sparks on the highway as it bounced like a low-rider wannabe.

My point here, brother, is that in every tear, there is a grain of wisdom...so long as you know to look for it.

Yes, there is joy in that. It's a victory to be celebrated provided you remember and respect the cost incurred.

CHAPTER 10

"We are here on Earth to fart around. Don't let anybody tell you any different." – Kurt Vonnegut

Of all the things I have experienced, which one had the most profound effect on my life?

That's a good question. I've not really considered it. It's like asking what ingredient of a shortbread cookie do I like best. All of them have their place, but when combined they make something unique and wonderful.

Right, you can't do that with a BLT. It's bacon all the way.

I think I'd have to say that at the time I experienced them they each were truly profound!

Well, more specifically, it is no longer a cluster of rabbit holes in my head. More accurately, it's a three-dimensional spider web…or a tag cloud on a website. It's all connected and they're all equally accessible.

Ah! Good catch! Yes, it is like the 3-D crystal snowflake I saw in my NDE when I was shown the interconnectivity of the

Universe. Maybe each of them appeared when I was ready? Now that I have had time to play with each one, I understand that they are all connected.

Yes, like a painter's palette, where each color has been revealed one at a time. With the primary colors revealed, I have now been shown how to mix them. To explore the potential...the nuance... that each can bring to a particular reality. Dude! That is an excellent analogy!

Right! Now I want to paint a happy little house here.

I wonder if the Universe is nothing more than the imagination of God. Or it may be more like an extraterrestrial, cosmic card game. I may have to write a book on that someday when I have more to say. Between the NDE, shared NDE, astral projection, and the beer-guzzling archangels, I have some cards to shuffle still.

Right. Back to your question.

Ghosts were first. And among all the phenomenal entities and experiences I've known...they were the least threatening. Also, it greased the wheels for what changes would come. I would say it was the perfect introduction of Transpersonal Psychology to a child.

Realizing that ghosts are just people without the meat suit took a couple of years. My first encounter with them after Grandpa was somewhat challenging as it was well outside the boundaries of my elementary school thinking and Catholic upbringing. At nine years old, I did not have a deep well from which to plumb and I sure as shit was not going to check in with the parental units again.

I knew ghosts from *Scooby-Doo* and *Casper*. I had heard of the Holy Ghost. I had read the comic *Ghost Rider*. Rather benign.

Then again, I had also heard the campfire story of a girl being picked up while walking next to a graveyard during an evening rainstorm. A driver stopped out of compassion and curiosity. She gave the driver instructions to get her home. Once there, the driver found the derelict home abandoned and the girl vanished from his car leaving behind a wet seat.

Yeah, my seat would be wet, too, if that happened to me. Should have worn the brown pants.

I guess I was young enough to just roll with it. And there was no fear...just caution. It was Grandpa and his love that set my expectations.

I did wonder. I wondered sometimes what would have happened if my parents had not put a damper on that exploration at such a young age. But I realized later that I was getting too hung up in the weeds. To move forward, I had to surrender to the probability that it happened the way it was supposed to happen...for this meat suit...in this reality. And, based on the concept of wisdom through pain, I needed to struggle.

Next? I separated the wheat from the chaff and moved on to the next step.

Excellent point. Perhaps it was necessary for ghosts to be the first experience so that my parents didn't freak out. And the fact that it was my mom's father—as opposed to the next-door neighbor who died, or some nature spirit having a visit—made it tolerable for everyone.

Because I got beatings and not an exorcism, you chucklehead.

Absolutely! Having out-of-body experiences—like remote viewing and astral projection—before I could even drive was an eye-opener. Discovering that part of me could go places and see things that my physical body could not do? Holy frijoles, El Batman!

To acquire knowledge without the use of my body was shocking! I thought it was just my imagination until I got confirmation. But once I settled into that reality, I became accustomed to it fairly quickly.

When it did slip out, I quickly covered my tracks with them. I told them it was a dream. It allowed me to speak a version of my truth that they could more easily deny with an explanation that made them feel better about it.

Because it met my needs at the time. People get inspiration all the time from unknown external forces. The word comes from *inspirare* which means 'to breathe or blow into.' Of course, *afflatus* means 'to blow,' but I'm pretty sure you don't want to go breathing that shit.

Grandpa had a saying about this: *Zieh meinen Fing.* It—it means pull my finger.

That old bastard would want to take a walk after a meal. He called it a nature walk or *Naturwanderung*. I would get distracted and fall behind him. I *know* he was waiting for that moment to let loose a growler.

You're right! Another bear reference! Let me tell you, that's a bear to be afraid of.

Cheers!

Let's be 100% here…I wanted the disassociation. It was partly escaping from my physical and emotional isolation, partly challenging my dictatorial father without the vehicle of peanut butter, and partly satisfying my insatiable curiosity. And, it's been said that Scorpios are drawn to esoteric knowledge so…

Right, why fight it?

I was in my late 20s when the Reiki turned on—so ghosts, astral projection, remote viewing were all "ordinary" to me by then. But the discoveries revealed by Reiki were both unreal and exciting. I just had to get out of my own way first.

What I mean is that it took awhile for my ego to get out of the way. I was doing it like a parlor trick. There was no respect...no solemnity.

I eventually came to the concept that I was not doing anything except setting an intention and becoming a funnel. I heard it described at a powwow once as becoming a 'hollow bone.' There is no technique or training necessary, except for just getting out of the way. But we all have busy minds and have certain proclivities that society has put upon us. So some may resonate with Reiki, while others will be drawn to Therapeutic Touch, and still others will prefer a 'laying on of hands.'

You are not doing anything. You are a passenger while allowing Reiki, or whatever noun you prefer, to pass through you and into the recipient. It is the recipient who decides what to do with that energy. It is they who are doing the healing. You are just a conduit of the energy for them to access and distribute as they see fit.

I'm just the jumper cables, broheim. It's the battery that matters.

What's it like? It's sitting completely still and quiet. My ego bounces around a bit and then steps aside while something sacred passes through. It feels like daydreaming. Occasionally, I see geometric symbols and colors, and I feel the energy...the voices of ascended masters.

I have tapped into a group who I used to call 'My Usual Suspects.' Later, while astral projecting, I was introduced to them as the White Brotherhood.

HA! No, not those assholes. Quite the opposite, actually. Imagine a group comprised of Gandalf, Merlin, Dr. Strange, Mother Theresa, and the like—from this Earth and other

"Earths"—who choose to resonate with the individual practitioner's energy.

They are not constrained by time, distance, race, religion, nor any other artificial construct that gives the illusion of division. They have been here in some capacity, seen the artificial burdens we are enslaved by, and have compassionately decided to reach back and help humanity where they can.

Physiologically, it can be as minute as my hands growing warm. It can be inexplicable—becoming drenched in sweat and radiating so much heat that the person sitting next to me begins freaking out. It can be a bit disconcerting at first, but once you relax into the process it is a magnificently euphoric experience.

Ha-ha-ha! Yeah, kinda like a spiritual orgasm. I'll drink to that!

I have hundreds of examples. But some things I cannot explain; I don't have the vocabulary to explain the totality of the experience. I just know they happened...and I surrender to the mystery.

OK. I once facilitated stopping an asthma attack from three time zones away as I mentioned earlier.

I also facilitated resetting a dislocated bone without touching it.

And I helped to clear a haunted house.

The first may have been a placebo effect as I had already treated the person at another time in the past. Regardless, this person felt better. That was one reason why I was so emphatic about practicing it on a hospital floor. Placebo or not, the person felt better and that was the goal in that moment.

In the second example, the bone was in a domesticated animal, so the placebo effect could not have been in play according to conventional thinking.

And lastly, the family reported the house as being peaceful after I had a conversation with the spirit, gave them some Reiki, and sent them toward the light.

Uncovering my past lives and discovering that I was not exploring all that life had to offer was a bit of a disappointment. Discovering the totality of my soul's mission—to explore the construct of abandonment—sucked ass!

Hell yes, for a long damn time!

Because I had this idea: I thought I was suffering as much as I had because I was about to ascend. In my mind, I had absorbed and transmuted so much pain in this life that I had filtered more than my ration of shit; I was going to be rewarded with coming home to stay. This sin-eater was friggin full.

Yeah, I was hoping to get off this ball of mud sometime soon. I have more friends over there than here. Lots more.

What does that say about being here? Sadly, the Earth is rife with opportunities to be cast aside when you are different. It's been said that when the world is blind, the one-eyed man is King. But what they don't mention is what it means to be King and to truly see one's environment.

Yes. Uneasy lies the head that wears the crown…or something like that.

Yes, the horrors. But, also the miracles. With the pain also came a sense of wonder. It then led me to a process of reintegration called soul fragment retrieval. It is a common shamanic practice known by many indigenous peoples. For me, I relished the fact that I was blending astral projection, past life regression, and Reiki into a single process.

Why? It was empowering as fuck!

My first projection backward was to the lifetime of the sea captain. I introduced my current self to my former self, and then coached him through his dying process while enveloping him in Reiki. It was paradigm-shattering. It was challenging to accept...at first.

Why?

Dude...I was projecting my consciousness into the past and energetically weaving together the concept of linear past lives. In my mind's eye, individual strands of The Self were becoming intertwined. The illusion of separate lives evaporated like a mythical mirage...like the dancing air above a desert highway.

I guess that means I was becoming stronger. Maybe wiser?

Stronger because it allowed me to sort abandonment and hopelessness into two different categories.

Abandonment is a situation; the pain of hopelessness is an emotional response to that abandonment. More specifically, it is an emotion I can choose, or not choose, to associate with that situation.

I chose to make the pain my purpose, and in doing so, it became more tolerable. Religion does the same thing. I can't tell you the number of times my grandma would respond to my childhood whining with the phrase, "Offer it up to God."

My despair, partially dissociated from my abandonment, became muted. That allowed me to absorb the energy of the lesson that was nested within the abandonment.

Well, it's a good feeling to go from "Woe is me" to "WOW is me!"

Cheers!

Yeah, lets reload. What's your choice?

Deep Sea Diver...OK. Dark rum, light rum, hi-octane rum, lime juice. What else am I missing?

Lime syrup and orange liqueur.

Shake with ice and served over rocks? Yeah, let's do that!

I'm glad you didn't order a piña colada. Never developed a taste for coconut after a college mishap with a coconut rum mix.

Roll how you want, my friend. Drink all the milky nut juice you want. Not my place to judge. Still, I may offer you a breath mint.

Well, 24/7, it's either on your breath or on your mind.

OK, OK...I drink almond milk. I guess we both like milky nut juice. You just like yours bigger, hairier, and from exotic locations.

Well, I'm a former Catholic and I like mine from smaller, hairless nuts.

Yeah, there's nothing redeeming down this road. Let's jump back to the original discussion.

To your health, brother.

Yes, abandonment...and the optional choice of pain...which I still choose.

Fuck yeah, it hurt. It still hurts! But rather than committing suicide and losing all the lessons, knowledge, and headway I have made this far, I asked my guides for a time out. I asked my angels to put me in a bubble for a while.

Without a wife, children, siblings, parents, friends, or a religious construct to share my load, I just needed time occasionally to rest. I still do.

Typically, within 24 hours, I get a reprieve in some fashion. I recover and I keep moving.

Thank you for your sympathy. Yeah, I used to see it as victimization. One thing Catholics know how to do is carry a cross! But I realized this was just a lesson. It was also a lesson of my own choosing while I was in a pre-corporeal state, so I bear the responsibility of both the pain and the reward. That realization dialed down my feeling of victimization; other lessons were then soon presented.

My pain is my gain. And, if my story helps others, then it is a gift, too.

The primary lesson is that this is the process of my soul's maturation. It is a maturation that requires numerous lifetimes. It's an awareness that not everyone has but probably should.

My growing pains are something I had selected before I arrived in the physical world. My pain became...sacred. And, it became separate—most of the time—from the weight of any particular life event.

I was just thinking that! The American Indian ritual of the sun dance. Pain is the key that opens the door to spiritual enlightenment. It facilitates a dissociative state. Once you recognize the pathway you can also recognize keys to that doorway other than pain.

Well, that is a larger issue. Mushrooms, LSD, ayahuasca, opioids–they are all illegal. But they have not legislated away meditation, prayer, fasting, and hypnosis. They, too, are doorways to perception.

The other lesson? I discovered I was a genius.

No, seriously.

Go ahead, laugh. It borders on the absurd, I know. But here is the simple rationale in my head.

I learned while studying The Silva Method that when a regular person and a genius sit next to each other on a train they are not dissimilar.

OK, when they sit at a bar, then. The difference is that the genius has learned, or earned, how to use their mind in ways that others do not. I have learned how to use my mind in ways that others do not. Ergo, I am a genius.

Yeah, my Latin is rusty, but I remember *cum hoc, ergo propter hoc.* And I know that it's bullshit. Just because one thing follows another doesn't mean one caused another. If I fart in bed before my alarm goes off that doesn't mean my fart caused the alarm to go off.

Oh, trust me...I get it. Farts are funny. Hell, I got Dutch-ovened by my 75-pound dog last week. It was alarming and it got me out of bed for damn sure.

Dude, I think she ate skunk and burning tires.

If we define a "genius" as someone who uses their mind differently than most people do, then I am a genius.

OK, I think I am smart. I have degrees in Music, English, and Nursing. I have a patent, I have written books, and I have helped bring several new drugs to market. But intelligence is only part of the equation.

Wisdom. Wisdom is the other part of the equation. It is a force multiplier.

Because, as I mentioned earlier, one's reach should not exceed their grasp.

Just because you have an open carry permit, it doesn't mean you should walk into a bank with your pistol in hand.

Dude, knowledge is more dangerous than a drawn weapon, given the right—or wrong!–circumstances. Thank Goddess I did not live in the village of Salem 400 years ago.

I digress. I am a genius in my own mind for two reasons.

First of all, I have an awareness of my soul's development which I have never had before now. In this space-time, while incorporated into this current iteration, I became aware that I have amassed thousands of individual life experiences through a dozen of live times. Somehow, I achieved critical mass and a metaphysical equivalent of singularity. I also achieved transpersonal awareness. I am, simultaneously, my physical body and my spiritual body.

People say they are a spiritual being having a human experience, but I can also say I am a unicorn, a Pegasus, or a horny equine. Just because I claim it doesn't mean I'm capable of comprehending it.

My past lives have moved from my supraconsciousness into my conscious life. I am both a corporeal being with a finite life span and an energetic being that is immortal. Beyond that, I have reached out, made contact, and shared in those lifetimes. Just as a driver moves from a broken-down vehicle to an operational one, my soul moves from one body to the next.

Think of it this way: In every lifetime, you are given a different octave to play on a piano. With each life, you temporarily forget that you had the previous octave, so you focus on the new one before you. Then, one day, you have this epiphany; you remember. Before you now stands a grand piano with all 88 keys. All that you are, all that you know, and all that you can become, have now grown exponentially.

That, in and of itself, is grounds for being a genius.

But you are missing the second part. The only thing I've mentioned so far is the knowledge.

Here comes the wisdom.

You have to play jazz.

In this incarnation, it is the first time I have held the tools, or abilities, to intentionally direct my soul's progress on a conscious level. The walls between my various states of consciousness are thinning.

Yes, reality is grounded in perspective.

I believe this is the first time my soul and my corporeal form are on the same page. For the first time, my soul's lesson plan is illuminated across the entire spectrum of consciousness. From my soul group to my meat suit, brother.

And the sexy part is that I have both the tools and the tenacity within this meat suit to do some amazing things.

Fuck yeah, I'll drink to that!

So, now I have the 88 keys in front of me. The musical riff I have been examining—abandonment—is something I have played in several lives, or in several keys.

Jazz is when you take the riff and you bend it, stretch it, and invert it. You beat it into submission and then you are beaten by it. And, when you have done with it all you can, you hand it off to the next physical iteration.

No, I am not offended, and I totally understand why you ask. I have never taken LSD or mushrooms. I've smoked enough pot to fill a pillowcase, but nothing more. You are on point though. Those are well-documented on-ramps onto the highway of Transpersonal Psychology.

But now that I think about it, I don't know...maybe someone in my ancestral lineage has taken those things. If so, there may be a genetic memory encoded in my DNA that I was able to activate. If not, then perhaps I activated soul-memory encoding. Or could it be that I had the video game equivalent of 'Achievement Unlocked' and my brotherhood inspired new information into me? That is a good mental chew toy to gnaw on.

This also generates another question. What is the *axis mundi* of knowledge: the brain, the DNA, or the soul?

Ha! You're right. Another book to write. But I should fully explore that thought?

I should set that intention, project back to those previous selves, and ask them.

Right, I could project forward and ask the same questions. I know future life progression is out there, but I have not tried it more than two or three times.

I haven't worked through all my past lives in the same detail as the captain. For some, I have only scratched the surface. But once I discovered what I was working on—the common thread among the lifetimes—I stopped.

As I mentioned before, I don't want to get into the weeds too much. I need to live this lifetime without getting lost in the rear-view mirror of this lifetime or any other. And there is something else...

What if my future self is an asshole?

You laugh, but seriously, in all this activity... in all that I have shared with you... I have left out a variable... a catalyst, perhaps.

At some point in my explorations, I settled myself and prepared for another past life projection. I surrendered my will and, instead, I asked to be guided to the lifetime that would benefit me the most. I was directed to my current life and my own childhood. I landed in my Grandpa's backyard right in front of my 4-year-old self.

Dude, it is by far the hardest life to navigate. The emotional noise I need to wade through is more...dense. Sometimes it's like trying to walk upstream against a strong current. Other days, it's like trying to wear white painter's overalls while standing behind a sneezing cow.

Seriously, you've never seen that? I told you before, man, it's like a blast from a shit shotgun. Maybe Jackson Pollack's muse was named Bessie?

Dude! You keep spitting your drink like that and they are going to make you wear a bib.

Again, I've never tried to put it into words. Leapfrogging in your own childhood is challenging. I guess I would describe it as trying to perform surgery on yourself. Maybe that's what Hippocrates meant by saying, "Heal thyself."

Quantum Leap? Yeah, I remember watching that TV show, but I don't remember if he ever leapt back into his *own* life. If he did, I imagine he did so to heal a childhood wound. But you've touched on something I have wrestled with for a while now.

Here's the catalyst part of the equation: When I asked to be shown where I need to direct my projection, what, or who, directed me to my childhood? Was it my own soul or was there some external force—an unseen spiritual Sherpa—that directed me?

I don't have an answer. It's yet another mental chew toy that I occasionally gnaw on. It may be one of those mysteries I just need to accept and move on.

You're probably right. It will be revealed when I am ready.

The delicious problem is I have so many avenues to explore that I don't linger on just one for too long. Other external forces in this plane of existence also divert my attention.

I'm buffeted by many external forces: ghosts, spirits, elementals, spirit guides, off-world etheric entities, entities in my Silva laboratory, higher beings like Saint Germain and Archangel Michael. And these are just the ones I have personally encountered in this dimension. If we go into projecting into other realities or into the extra-dimensional space between realities…sorry, dude. I'm rambling.

I'm sorry. I know this is a lot to be throwing at you. And I do not expect you to believe a word I'm saying.

All I'm asking is for you to entertain the idea that your reality and my reality are different because our experiences are different and that neither of us is wrong. Your reality is right for you; mine is right for me. Reality is like water—solid for some, liquid for others.

My point is this: Reality is a moving river made up of presumed facts and you can never grasp the same water twice. Facts change. Ask author Graham Hancock, scientist Francis Crick, or journalist Nick Pope.

OK, ghosts and spirits we've covered. Elementals are spirit energies, too, but they have never been in human form. Sprites, fairies, wood elves, mountain lights, and so on, fall into this category.

Another rung on the spiritual ladder of energy is our ancestors. Their energy is close to human but vibrates at a higher rate. As well-meaning as they are, they are not the authority and are still subject to human emotional states. These states can affect their thinking process.

Next are the Reiki Masters of past, present and future. When I am in healing mode, they are front and center. Their collective knowledge is vastly superior to that of humans, but they have been human. They have a frame of reference that's relevant to my situation while using Reiki.

Spirit guides and other tutors are in the realm of even higher energy. They can still access the human plane of existence without too much effort. In this space are the group of healers I mentioned before who identify themselves as the White Brotherhood. When situations arise where more than "healing" is going on, they are there for me, such as when I'm engaged in activities like clearing places where elementals or other nonhuman things are present.

Bridging the gap between the White Brotherhood and angels are the Ascended Masters. I used to think they were ascended humans, but I have also encountered beings in that group that don't have the same vibration. So, my verdict is still out.

In short, they have some affiliation with the human animal, but I am unsure whether they have ever been human. Perhaps they were humans from a different timeline or different civilization. They may have shared consciousness with a human host, but they are more energy than anything else. Another way of looking at this is beer. Pabst and Sam Adams both sell beer, but I'm sure you will agree that they are not identical.

The next level of energy I have experienced is occupied by an energy who identifies himself as Saint Germain. He first appeared to me in human form; now I see him as a purple, geometric figure. In fact, I have never seen him otherwise since his first introduction.

Archangel Michael occupies the highest energy level I have ever experienced in the physical. He showed up at my Master level Reiki attunement. He also shows up when I need to kick things up a few notches.

I don't want to elaborate just yet, but I am almost there. Just a couple of minutes more.

In my mind, I have a construct that I call the laboratory which was facilitated by my work with The Silva Method. In this place, Reiki Masters, the White Brotherhood, and Ascended Masters will come and go depending on my need and ability to comprehend. Occasionally, I ask for a particular group. Most recently, they are already there waiting for me.

These are all the energetic entities I have encountered; they ascend and descend the energetic ladder as the needs of any given situation dictate.

Yes, I have been challenged by some negative counterparts, but I have had the appropriate help to handle it. What worries me though is the number of physical entities on this level...the ones currently on Earth, but not of it.

Extraterrestrials.

Yup, extraterrestrials.

It is a threshold that few will cross.

Again, I don't expect you to believe in them. I am merely asking you to believe that my reality is different from yours.

Based on my astral projections, they're real, they're here, and I'm pretty sure they think they own the joint.

I've been tracking them for a few years now. They've been here since before humankind existed and they have been cultivating the human animal since Day One, which was a few hundred thousand years ago.

Like I said, my reality is my own. It's no more valid or invalid than yours. But "factual" perception is the foundation of the collective reality. And the more I investigate, the more my facts change.

I know. It is a lot to grasp. It has taken me more than a decade to build a semi-cohesive narrative. It's hard to trace a single thread through a throw rug big enough to cover an aircraft carrier.

With all the things I have just said, I will now answer your question. I think the one thing that had the most profound impact on me was my near-death experience because it affirmed some of my long-standing suspicions, opened up my mind to new paths, and planted a new operating system in my head. Since then—"then" being 2011—an abundance of new, executable files have been popping open starting with the singing of gratitude by Nature.

Like expensive lingerie, it's a gift that keeps paying dividends, brother.

Guitars, Cigars and Tiki Bars

CHAPTER 11

The path of spiritual enlightenment is this—don't be a dick.

Lessons like these will never be taught in school but they are imperative to learn. Unfortunately, some need to live the lesson to learn it. Lessons like:

> Don't eat a bean burrito if there is even the slightest chance of having sex.
>
> Don't splice your cable feed from your neighbor—especially if they are a cop.
>
> Don't have the Twister bedspread out on the first date.
>
> Don't feel confident that you can make it to the next gas station...whether you need gas or to drop the deuce.
>
> Do not engage with fresh jalapeños regardless of whether or not you are the "chopper" or the "choppee", because of the burrito rule. The sex is memorable—but for all the wrong reasons.

Never call them granny panties. Never. Ever, ever, ever, ever, ever.

Nothing below her neck looks like her mother's. Or her sister's.

When she shows you how to fold something, that is the only officially sanctioned way to fold it. Amen.

A circular saw is an inappropriate Christmas gift. Same goes for a vacuum cleaner.

Whoever said that great stories start with bad decisions is freakin brilliant.

Hmm… one of my best decisions… setting up recordings of the shows you want to see some weekend. Then give her control of the remote and actually watch those shows with her. She will lose her damn mind.

Seriously! She will tell her friends, who will first think she is lying, and then tell her how extraordinarily lucky she is. Her friends will be envious. She will be happy. You will be rewarded in ways that you will think it's your birthday. Your name will be whispered reverently to her sisters at Thanksgiving dinner.

Yes, cheers to birthday sex! Huzzah!

Where shall we go from here? Circle back or forward?

More on Ascended Masters?

I think they do the heavy lifting in the physical realm.

Angels are pure energy. Ascended Masters are more in tune with the business of earthly existence. Angels know of free will, but Ascended Masters have lived with those decisions and the results thereof…for good or bad.

Well, angels would not "get" the Hitler question, whereas an Ascended Master would.

Never seen that one happen?

Sometimes, when I go to metaphysical discussions, I hear the "Hitler" question: "Why would an all-loving God permit someone like Hitler to exist?"

Sometimes it's asked as a "gotcha" question—as if defending Hitler would be an abomination to God and, therefore, invalidate anything a speaker would say or had already said.

I have seen speakers tiptoe around this issue to keep that sleeping dog on the porch. I am not a tiptoe kind of person. Rather than skirt the issue, I prefer to walk up to the dog with both a piece of bacon and a stick.

Although mean-spirited, there is a kernel of truth in the "gotcha" with respect to Evil in the world. I have never been asked this question directly, but if I were ever given the opportunity, I would answer it in the following fashion: Hitler was an Ascended Master.

Right! And boom goes the dynamite!

OK, maybe I wouldn't lead with that because the emotional shock would close the ears of those who probably most need to hear it. So let me start again and ease into it with the bacon.

Before my NDE, I had read Dr. Brian Weiss and Dr. Michael Newton, and was doubtful of their findings. Who can really understand the process of ascending into that energetic state some call Heaven? Better yet, who can stand in the presence of eternal wisdom and pure love that is both unyielding and unconditional, and then come back to this shit-hole commonly known as Earth, and be able to clearly relate the experience to others? It's impossible.

Then, I had an NDE.

When I was back home, there was no judgment. Well, there was no judgment from God or Source or whatever proper noun you prefer. There was a huge sense of disappointment from within myself because I was embarrassed by my earthly transgressions. They had been laid bare for all to see.

All of the events of my life were there for review; there was no hiding. Childhood shoplifting, teasing kids on the school bus, sneaking the car out after midnight, cheating on an exam...anything that one may have done which is not in alignment with the highest and greatest good is there for review. So too, though, are the moments when I succeeded.

In my despair, I hung my head in shame before Source.

In reply to my shame, I felt a huge surge of unconditional love! HUGE! In my mind I heard a voice say, "You take yourself too seriously and you do so far too often. I have made you a playground. Go play." To be washed in that love made me want to do only one thing. I wanted to demonstrate my appreciation. That memory still brings me to tears more than a decade later.

I have done things in my past of which I am still ashamed. We all have. It's part of the human experience. But to know that I am loved regardless of what I have done, or how I look, or what value I have contributed to society, gives me great comfort. As a child and a spouse, unconditional love was simply not there for me. My experience tells me that I may turn from God, but God will never turn from me. In my opinion, Hell is not a place. It is the lack of awareness of one's connection to God. To paraphrase Anne Frank, the Sun shines—even in the darkest night.

My personal experience also tells me that, as a soul, I still have free will. As master of my soul I can remain as a spiritual consciousness, surf the Akashic Records, and read about all sorts of adventures attempted by my former or future self. I can also choose to hang out with my soul group.

My soul group is like a community theater troupe. We all know each other and have been friends forever. We occasionally decide to put on a show and try out a role. We then change roles just to keep things interesting and to develop or enhance our skills. Over time, we may learn to run the sound board, use the follow spot, make costumes, and—as all Hollywood actors say—"All I really want to do is direct."

We will have mastered all the variables. And in this metaphor, we all become directors, eventually. We ascend to such a high frequency that we can again become one with God.

Stick with me, I'm about to bring this home.

So let's say I am a soul and my soul name is Trevor. Trevor has been around the block and has evolved to the point where he now chooses to learn some very hard lessons. It is a path some philosophers refer to as the trauma of enlightenment. There are friends in Trevor's soul group who love him enough to be the facilitators of that trauma. Whether you are licking a flagpole in winter, running on wet floors with scissors, or being murdered because of your religion, color or political ideology, a lesson will be learned.

Here's where I tie this all together.

While in Heaven, in between "incarnate" states, the facts are these: God loves me regardless. I want to be more integrated into God. Free will is always present.

Once on Earth, it is expected that ego will distract us from God's presence. God wants humanity to grow and mature into self-actualized, self-aware entities. Sometimes that means living in an illusion where God seems nonexistent.

As a human being, Adolf Hitler was a racist egomaniac who came into power over a broke and broken country. Post-World War I sanctions had left the economy in ruins; paper money was used for kindling. The national ego had been battered and the population was desolate. It was an identity crisis, a power vacuum, and a series of improbable events all at once…a perfect storm awaiting a trigger.

Now, allow me to offer another perspective—Hitler's soul's perspective—and using your human morals will not work here.

OK, back to Trevor. Let's say I'm an old soul, an Ascended Master, in fact. I have lived hundreds of lifetimes and have mastered the human experience to the point that I only go down to Earth when heavy lifting, such as a shift of consciousness, is needed.

While the lives of Gandhi and Mother Theresa shifted the consciousness of some, there needed to be a shift for all of mankind. A shift of Old Testament proportions. And if you are familiar with the story of Noah or Passover, you know that Old Testament God uses Archangel Azrael as a way to get shit done.

Archangel Azrael is known as the Angel of Death.

Remember, we're still with Ascended Master Trevor. So one day, he's hangin' with his spiritual and angelic homies when God pops in to visit. "Yo, Trevor, time for a shift of consciousness—and it's gonna be huge. Not just county, country or continent, but the entire freakin' world."

While the rest of the homies are thinking they need to get out the umbrellas again, Trevor thinks this would be a great service to God and to all of God's beloved. Of course, Trevor wants to say yes to whatever the plan is.

But God warns Trevor there will be an enormous price. Millions will die a tragic death. Millions more will experience a degree of suffering like no other in human history. Remember, wisdom is knowledge with pain. Generations upon generations of those who survive this plan will focus their hatred on one human.

A legion of souls had already agreed to suffer this human fate before returning to Earth again. Their suffering, while tragic, would inspire the rest of humanity—like that of a child willing to die for their parent. However, in order for this tumult and ascension to occur, there would need to be a catalyst.

This catalyst, God said, would be a human who would be reviled throughout the rest of human history. This human being would be so reviled that they would compare him to the anti-Christ. As one so close to returning to God, the Ascended Master would have to shoulder an enormous burden and agree to be the human representation of the antithesis of God.

As a soul, I literally cannot imagine being the trigger for the killing and suffering of tens of millions of people—the instrument of destruction of so many of God's beloved creations. While standing before God, I can only see love, feel love, and be moved by the spirit of love.

Trevor sees love, too, but in that love he sees a lesson. He sees a path by which those who are lost can find their way back to God. He sees a plan that can return lost children back to their Father. For this to work, though, he must agree to be the focus of humanity's anger, hate, and outrage, for dozens of generations.

As a soul, I think it would be my love for God, the love of humanity's evolution, and the desire to please God that would convince me to agree to exercise my free will and become a human being that would be reviled. A truly powerful and ancient soul would be the only one equipped to shoulder such a burden. Looking into the mind of Creation, and the heart of infinite love, I would say yes to God. I would be this catalyst. I would agree to be born Adolf Hitler.

Those who were physically present during and after World War II witnessed an evolutionary spike across the board. Women got out of the kitchen and became more autonomous. The GI Bill made college available to thousands. The list of inventions is exhaustive: radar, sonar, jet propulsion, computers, synthetic materials, genetics, atomic energy...the list goes on. Never in all of recorded history had humanity's industry has been dedicated to a singular resolve. Stop Hitler.

In Hamlet, Act 2 Scene 2, Hamlet is vexed and makes the comment, "...there is nothing either good or bad, but thinking makes it so." Prior to World War I, my great-grandparents left their homeland in southern Germany for America and her isolationist principles. Those isolationist tendencies eroded over the next two decades. As a result, many of my ancestors became soldiers, and cousins would kill cousins. Surviving cousins would have survivor's guilt. Is this good or bad?

Some died bleeding on winter battlefields while others died decades later in warm beds. Is this good or bad?

Here's a more contemporary query. A Muslim Iraqi soldier, who has lost his hand in battle, has it replaced with a bionic prosthesis made by a Jewish American physician. Is this good or bad?

My point to the "gotcha'" people is this: At the soul level, no individual is good or bad; no action is good or bad. Every action undertaken by any individual is an experience that makes that individual a wiser soul and brings him—or her—closer to God's infinite wisdom. Better yet, when any of us love another in this *opera buffa* called life, we are drawn closer to God.

In the nonphysical, non egoic state of spiritual existence, you resonate at such a high vibrational rate that you hang out with angels and masters. In the presence of God, there is love—perpetual, unremitting, pervasive love. Just below the surface of that love, you feel the wisdom. In this rapturous mix of love and wisdom, there is also a sense of joy. You can see it, feel it, merge with it, and be moved by the spirit of love while in His presence.

So as an infinite soul with no human ego or situational morality, and while looking into God's loving gaze, what challenge would you be willing to take up? Within the majesty of this exponential love, would you exercise free will and become a human being? The love God has for His creations, and His desire for humanity's evolution, is measured in eons. What is one single human lifetime when the unit of measure is infinity? In that envelope of love, what hazards would you be willing to dare?

Welcome to Humanity 101: The Earth Files.

Eleven million people, including six million Jews and a million children, were exterminated. Eleven million souls elevated humanity in awareness, compassion, morality, and coordinated a global reach toward a greater good. In less than two decades, how many millions have been elevated by their one-time sacrifice?

The person, Adolf Hitler, nearly destroyed the Jews, the disabled, Gypsies, and homosexuals. His reputation still haunts a country—even a world. Ascended Master Trevor, an instrument of God and in the guise of a human, united mankind in a way no other person on Earth ever has. I'm not so sure that even Jesus—or John Lennon—could make such a claim.

Dude, you have been more than kind to listen to all the stuff I have been laying out here. You probably need to go.

No, I've taken up too much of your time. You've been very, very gracious with your time and tolerance. I don't want to impose upon you any longer. Your wife will be pissed.

You're divorced, too? Well, you may not need to account for your time, but I still don't want to impose more than I already have. But I am supremely grateful for your willingness to suspend belief and listen to the ramblings of an old fart.

No, on the contrary, I've enjoyed our time together. I have cracked so many smiles today that my face hurts! A chimp with a hand mirror has got nothing on me, bro.

If I may ask, how long ago were you divorced?

Go figure. I've been divorced about that long, too. Have you discovered the post-divorce secret yet?

OK, beyond not eating Cheesy Poofs while masturbating?

The power of Control-Alt-Delete. The power of rebooting.

Divorce is a shattered, stained-glass window that you should rebuild.

The individual pieces are scattered but do not break, and each colored bit is a part of you. The blessing is in discovering that you can reconstruct the window from those component parts without the constraints of familial, societal, or religious expectations.

I was able to build a new me and there wasn't anyone there to tell me I couldn't. After years of constraint, it was a godsend.

Well, for me, it was an amazing part of the traditional human experience.

Yes, divorce is just another human story. And an old one, to boot. But I moved a few hundred miles away and began my rebuilding process with essentially the same physical things I had when I graduated college. I was poor in possessions but rich in opportunities. I had the freedom to create a better version of me and I chose to make it so. I consider it my hero's journey.

I would say it was on par with becoming music.

Yes, when I remembered having become music, that was an example of a file folder opening. One minute, I had no recollection. The next minute, I had a full set of memories, emotions, and experiences available to me. Divorce was a slow-motion experience of the same revelation.

You're right. I do sometimes wonder what folders I have in my head that have not yet been opened. Again, with everything I have experienced, I'd say the near-death experience was the most profound.

Too late for a short answer, I know, but another benefit was that it took me off the path of chasing the American dream, or nightmare, of materialism. I stopped chasing bigger paychecks and additional letters behind my name. I stopped a process I called my "soft suicide." I manned up and made ready for the inevitable divorce and the shit storm and sunshine that would follow.

My "soft suicide" was my attempt to get out of my marriage in an honorable way by slowly killing myself. Getting my blood sugar over 500 and my weight over 400.

I was genetically predisposed to have heart disease and diabetes. After my NDE, I ate shitty food like bacon, fried eggs, and pancakes every day for months. I stopped taking my meds. I stopped my hobbies of carpentry and book collecting, and lost myself in daytime TV. I wrote goodbye letters and even planned my own funeral.

From the outside, it looked like sloth. But what I dearly wanted was to go back to unconditional love. There was absolutely none in my home.

To be fair, my wife married one guy, and when I came back from the coma I was not that guy anymore. Our energies were absolutely incompatible from that point forward.

I can now see that we were destined to cross paths. In a previous lifetime, we killed each other. In this one, we rescued each other. With that karmic bill paid, we needed to go different ways.

Oh, once I got home from the hospital, I was in full launch mode. I had decided on moving from Indiana to New Zealand. I had applied for a visa and been bumped to the top of the queue because I was both a nurse and an experienced pharmaceutical researcher.

No, I never went. I realized I was running away from myself.

It sucked, but I was going to have to learn a new jazz riff. I was going to have to pivot...again. Actually, I was going to have to pivot no matter where I lived. So rather than running to the other side of the world, I moved to a place where I could recover physically and fiscally...and be near good blues music: Chicago.

It was a good move. I got to rediscover myself after having abdicated my own self-worth. I remember being so proud when I bought myself new underwear and socks and did not need permission to do so. I felt like such a renegade!

I was able to explore things I had not been afforded earlier. I published short stories. I learned nature survival skills. I explored Unity and Unitarianism. I created my own company. I began singing again. I was the hero of my own story because I was also the director.

Joseph Campbell is perhaps the most famous, but he is certainly not the first. Literature is choking on the ubiquitous conceit where a protagonist enters into a task unwillingly, is separated from kith and kin, makes a perilous journey fraught with unseen dangers, and implying certain death. The hero survives those experiences and, once completed, returns changed for the better for both themselves and all who are in their circle.

Yes! Just like Joseph Campbell's *Hero with a Thousand Faces*. You understand. This is supposedly the work where George Lucas was inspired to create Luke Skywalker.

I think Jar Jar came from bad gas station sushi.

Ever read the *Epic of Gilgamesh*? Same story. Ever heard of *The Prophet* or *The Alchemist*? Same story. There are 39 centuries between the stories of Gilgamesh and Jesus, and they have the same message. Osiris, Prometheus, Moses, Jesus, Muhammad, Siddhartha, Gandhi...

There are several variations, but I believe the unifying thread is that a man may seek to expand his horizons, but mankind will violently protect the status quo.

Civilization celebrates heroes but also fears them.

Think about it. In reality, the hero's return is marked by rejection—rejection by traditional support systems of family, friends and religion. They are rejected because they are changed.

There is no celebration. There are whispers of, "Why can't they go back to being who they were?"

It gets even more problematic.

Because the hero is bewildered by the collective support system's rejection. They see their own survival and subsequent shift as a friggin' miracle. But the collective's expectation is a return to conformity. It should be no surprise, then, when these individuals eventually present clinically as having PTSD. And by that measure, there are millions.

Who? The ten million Americans a year who reported having an NDE. The millions more who report an STE—a spiritually transformative experience. The thousands who report being abducted by aliens. And, of course, the soldiers who come back from a conflict. The fact is they all will present clinically with PTSD. And that is just Americans. The world, my friend, is changing faster than we can accommodate.

You think they're different?

OK, riddle me this. Of the aforementioned people, which ones experienced an event outside the traditional norms of society?

Right. All of them.

Which ones returned from that experience a changed person? Which ones have trouble reintegrating into society?

Yup. All of them.

Which ones feel like they can't talk about what happened to them? Which ones have a change in their views on religion or the government? Which ones become exhausted with trying to fit in and choose to commit suicide instead?

Yes, I am passionate about these people. I *am* one of these people. I've been diagnosed with complex PTSD.

One day at a time, brother. One day at a time.

Well, I can't speak for soldiers in this day and age. But I can speak for a subset of people who are under the umbrella term called Exceptional Human Experience.

Under that umbrella fit the NDE'ers, the near NDE'ers, and the STE'ers. Remember, more than 10 million Americans a year fall into this category. The numbers worldwide must be astonishing.

You're right. It is another example of critical mass.

The EHE'ers come back with a very specific set of changes. The most common changes include changes in values...typically a decreased interest in materialism. With that comes improved behavior and attitude toward others and a greater empathy and compassion for the planet.

Well, everyone could benefit from a greater sense of well-being.

Many have a change in their spiritual or religious views. Sometimes they become more or less fundamental, but the change is obvious to any outsider.

They also come back with a greater desire and capacity to learn, increased creativity, increased psychic awareness, and a greater sense of purpose.

Sure! On the surface, these seem to be beneficial changes. However, these changes, which may take others a lifetime to achieve, are relatively sudden and are oftentimes drastic. They can literally happen overnight to the experiencer. One minute they are sipping on a beer and debating the merits of a zero-radius lawn mower and the next they are selling Reiki imbued tomatoes online.

It is shocking! For all parties!

This change is often just as befuddling to the one experiencing it as it is to those who have known the individual before the change occurred. Imagine waking up some morning to discover that your computer's operating system has been updated to a version the public won't see for 100 years. Your RAM has been quintupled and your solid-state hard drive modified to a quantum drive. Your system files load just by thinking about them. All the original files are still there, but they look and feel very different.

The most astounding change is that the file structure method of organizing has been replaced with something that looks more like...

YES! That crystalline sphere of fire I saw when touring the Universe.

God's neural network? I don't know if I would go that far, but it is as good an explanation as any.

I can't tell you how happy it makes me that you were listening! Even more so that I was able to convey it in a way you understood!

Exactly. For some of us, there are hidden files that pop open days to years later. For those of us who have the "upgrade" forced upon us, it can cause true mental illness. The human animal can only adapt so fast. Processing a radical shift in reality can sure strip the gears.

Correct. Disclosure. I'm watching the Space Force story and trying to decide if it's because they can no longer hide the costs in the black budget or because they need to get the public narrative closer to the "secret" one.

That's why those around us struggle to understand our download. We are reworked on the inside while still keeping our old familiar meat suit. That struggle to reintegrate, to revert, to fit back into the old mold, results in reentry turbulence.

I think it has been in the zeitgeist long enough for people to grasp the feeling we have of wanting to return to Source. It's a homesickness with no solution. That loneliness is compounded by those who just flat out refuse to believe us, think we are angling for a buck, or think we need to see a mental health professional.

No, I don't disagree with you. This message can actually be a draw to those with certain pathologies. That's when the listener needs to practice discernment. Sadly, not many have the capability or inclination to do so. Mass media and our educational system do not encourage such cognitive autonomy.

As a clinical research professional and an NDE'er, I have a unique perspective among unique perspectives. I once sat in a room of clinicians who were deciding how best to test their NDE patients. After giving them a half hour to parry and thrust their ideas, I floated this tidbit out there.

"How do you propose to surreptitiously test a group of people who have demonstrated psychic abilities?" Silence followed.

Oh yeah! They can get their psychic abilities dialed up to 11. They can also experience increased sensitivity to electricity, chemicals, smells, sounds...pretty much anything this world generates. For a while, I used to walk under street lights at night. They would turn off right before I got to them and go back on after I passed.

Oh sure. It sounds magical until you realize you need a psychic HAZMAT suit to go to Wally World.

Dude, it can be hellish. Which is ironic when you consider you recently shared a reality sandwich with the Prime Mover. Thanks for the parting gift, Big G.

Reintegration has been reported to take seven years based on the data I've seen. However, some data show as high as 12 percent of experiencers can never thoroughly integrate an NDE; it is an ongoing process of growth, work, exploration, suffering, and learning.

Again, the diversity of responses I've read suggests that both the integration process and desired outcomes are never completely done. The process of integrating the experience is highly individualized and the task to which they are assigned may be a burden for the duration of their life.

So, yes, I got "The Message." The same message that nearly every other NDE'er gets.

No protracted book is necessary. I can sum it up very quickly: Don't be a dick. Yup. That simple.

Nah. The Ten Commandments, the Golden Rule, The Secret...any and all of them can be boiled down to that statement. Don't be a dick.

You're right. I guess the NLP version would be a *Bill and Ted* reference: Be excellent to each other.

HA! I like that. I don't know if John Lennon would have gotten as much airplay with "Don't Be a Dick" as he did with *Imagine*.

No, I don't think people are that way inherently. I think we are all at different points on the path. When we hear about ground that we've already covered, we can collectively nod in agreement. But when we get to the part of the narrative where we have no reference, we get scared.

There is a thin veneer of civility over civilization. Scare a person, all's well. Scare people and there is a collective skid mark on humanity's Hanes highway.

Scare you?

OK...we are not alone in the Universe. Nearly everyone who hears that nods in agreement.

Parse it differently: Extraterrestrials exist.

Did you hear that? That was thousands of minds slamming shut. For those who remain, I'll push the boundary.

Extraterrestrials existed in this solar system before Earth was populated with humanoids.

They exist in the solar system now. They exist on or in every planet in the solar system. They exist here on Earth—under mountains and underwater. Extraterrestrials exist, are invisible, and could be hiding in everyone's attic. Some of them walk among us because they look like us.

I get it. You stimulate the threat-based, fight or flight reflex...the reptilian brain...and your ability to think rationally is gone like a fart in the wind. If there is ever a "Disclosure," it will be with a small "D." I think humanity can handle a gradual reveal over a handful of years a whole lot easier than a handful of aliens landing on the White House lawn. I mean...you think our Immigration policy is screwed up now?

Nope. Not scary for me. I'm OK with either the big D or the little D. Wait, we're still talking about disclosure of ETs, right? Because there are enough of the other Big D's in Washington, DC.

They don't bother me because I have projected out to different planets and have met different entities...and they are like us. Strengths and weaknesses, predilections and prejudices, and striking a balance of intelligence versus wisdom just as we are doing. The only difference is magnitude and duration.

Nah, my religion was not affected by this information. If anything, it strengthened it. Just like the old gospel hymn: I gazed out in awesome wonder at the works thy hand hath made.

Really! How dare we limit God's ability of infinite expression by saying *Homo sapiens* is the pinnacle of life forms! It stinks, it leaks, it has a snot faucet turned upside-down over the food intake orifice and it breaks down in less than a century. Sorry God, you get a C-minus. Go back and try again.

Who's to say? Maybe God has been created in the image of man—by man. Humankind is a product not of God's image but of His imagination. And who's to say that God didn't get a subcontractor to do the light work? God may have drawn up the blueprints, but maybe those who seeded this place and other worlds have a 100,000-year lifespan.

Well, in the last 400 years, we've nearly doubled the expected life span. And technology is on an exponential curve. What will the next 200 years bring? Will we be cloning our bodies and uploading our consciousness into the next meat suit? Will technology make dying obsolete?

We are all struggling to be godlike. We just have different images of "God" in our head.

Really? You think a Jewish carpenter's son from Zero A.D. Nazareth was blond-haired and blue-eyed?

I love that movie line: "Not you, Fat Jesus."

We are becoming more godlike every day. We've created life by introducing electricity into a pool of amino acids. We are already creating cloned beings and beings from frozen eggs. We're unzipping and splicing DNA from one species to another and using viruses to inject foreign proteins. What will we be doing in 200 years? Where we now schedule a tooth extraction and take a day off afterwards, the next generation may go to a CRISPR clinic and have their genetic diabetes unzipped and replaced.

Yeah, I don't understand why so many people get their tits in a wringer over that concept. We'll probably be going to and populating the Moon...and the same thing on Mars, right? Guess what? That makes *us* the extraterrestrials. If we make it to another planet where the indigenous life is akin to our pre-Sumerian ancestors, then we are perpetuating the Ancient Alien theory.

So if another race has a 100,000-year head start, why is it so hard to believe? As long as we are *doing* the exploring, it's acceptable. When we are *being* explored, then it's crazy talk.

I think part of it is the unspoken fear that we will be treated in exactly the same way we have treated indigenous peoples when we discovered them...genocide with a dash of slavery.

No wonder people clam up. Karma can be a bitch, but she is only getting what she's owed…and being part Cherokee, I'm kinda looking forward to it.

I differentiate between the physical and the spiritual. While we have aliens running around on the physical plane, I think there are energetic beings, navigating energetic "Chutes and Ladders" when and where they're needed.

I think they are like some humans in the fact that they are compelled to help. Compelled…but not imposing upon our Free Will. We have to ask for help before they get involved.

Angels, Energetic Beings, enlightened human souls—all are here to teach, to help awaken the human spirit, and to help humankind rise to higher levels of consciousness. That message is usually well received. But if you exclude the student from the equation, then what the hell is the purpose for the teachers?

Well, if you buy into all of this, then beings with the opposite intent are here doing their thing. If you have saints and angels, then you have to have sinners and demons or there is no reason for them to exist. Reveal the message in that way and the room clears.

Look, no matter how crowded the universal stage becomes, we're all still trying to do the same thing. We are trying to achieve a more integrated sense of self. But we are distracted by greed, avarice, prejudice, ego, Cheesy Poofs, or our Netflix queue. Free will allows us to be distracted—and then we ignore our purpose. Even in that, there is a lesson.

Dude…there is no fun in fundamentalism.

No one lives in an amusement park. We go to be thrilled and distracted. Nor should we try to ride every single ride in the amusement park. At some point, we need to get back to our work.

Konstantin Stanislavski remarked that "there are no small parts, only small actors."

Well, your work is going to be different from mine because it plays to your soul's unique plan. From a big-picture perspective though, I think we all stand on the precipice of a quantum leap from both the biological and spiritual levels. I just don't know if this will be a leap forward or backward.

Dude. Changes aren't coming; they're *here*! Religious structures are falling apart, financial systems are unstable, facts are called opinions and opinions are called facts, The Earth itself is becoming more toxic daily. The Great Pacific Garbage Patch is two times bigger than Texas. A hundred million tons of radioactive water is sitting in tanks in Fukushima and there are untold millions that spilled into the Atlantic. Cesium has been found on the west coast in goat's milk... which means it is in the water table. The magnetic fields are slipping forcing airports to recalibrate where North really is. The sun is burping radioactive blasts. Even the area of the Universe we are spinning through is screwing with the Schumann Frequency and is changing the background frequency of space itself.

If your sphincter hasn't slammed shut, then you've got to get your nose out of your phone and into the world.

Agreed. It's hard because there are multiple systems of distraction. Like Plato kinda said, stop looking at the shadows, stop looking at the tchotchkes, and find the fire.

You can shout it from the rooftops, but the message gets hijacked by the end-of-times contingent selling their religion, heirloom seeds, or freeze-dried shit.

It dissolves into noise and chatter. All you can do is find your path and walk it like you mean it. Live your message and hope someone notices.

My reality? OK...here is where I plant my flag.

I, along with thousands of others, have been programmed for a variety of "future" activities including an awareness of my own soul contract. I am compelled to share these messages with others but I refuse to proselytize. Like a nurse or a well-meaning parent, I will tell you what I know and then I will surrender the outcome.

I move in the direction of greater self-awareness, greater concern for the welfare of planet Earth, and a greater sense of community with both humankind and other beings in the solar system.

My personal metamorphosis is part of the harbinger of the global transformation in human consciousness. As evidence, I offer the changes in the economic, political, educational, military, and religious institutions on Earth. Tried and true pillars of control will collapse from within. A new world order will be replaced with a collective humanitarian agreement in which our industry, science, and spirituality coexist harmoniously. Those that attempted to manifest the other New World Order will fade away either by conversion or conviction.

People like myself have been seeding the population for generations and will continue to do so until enough people wake up. Critical mass is closer than it has ever been. Our collective intention is to create physical and spiritual manifestations designed to influence the worldview of all humankind, so that they may discover and share this evolution with others.

In the meantime, you will need to bob and weave through people who are scared and want to remain in their fading reality. They will be as dangerous as a drowning swimmer. However, if you don't change, then you will be perfectly equipped for a world that no longer serves you.

Nope. I've never read Nietzsche, but I speak enough German to know what an *Übermensch* is.

No. I don't think that I am. I'm just a dude that may have broken his brain, likes tiki drinks, smokes an occasional cigar, and touches himself a bit more than necessary. But when I hear my own words, they don't sound crazy. They sound like I have hope in the face of some pretty damn long odds.

At some point the numbers of experiencers will increase to a tipping point where society will be changed. Look up the Peace Intention Experiment. It only takes 1.1 percent of the local population to affect changes in the behavior of the rest of the group.

That's the beauty of it, though. Not everyone needs to go through pain or have an NDE. The capacity is already within each and every one of us. We all have the capacity to be psychic...in touch with Source...or just friggin woke! It only requires choice.

Anyway, that was part of my NDE download. But it is also part of my general observations having been around for a few decades. There are people who are awake and people who are asleep. It bears repeating that some of the awakened are in learning mode. Some are in refinement mode like video game players who are replaying a level to get a better score.

Some of us here who got the download are at this point in time "spiritual paramedics." There is a bumpy ride before us, as with any transition, and those who are asleep are going to struggle.

In short, some will change for the better. And some will have to come back and try again.

Right! Let go or be dragged.

No! You. Are. Not. Alone. Remember that everyone has a team of helpers in the spiritual realm. Some are specifically for you; some are for when you require specialized help. If you need help, ask. Ask and ye shall receive.

Dude, it's not some spiritual game of duck, duck, goose. I can't just tap people on the head and change their minds. Free will is free will, and if you are addicted to the comic opera of your reality, I can't change that.

I can lead a horse to water but I can't make them think.

Only you can fix you. All I can do is show you how I did it for me. After that, I can support you, sympathize with you, and empathize with you. I can feed you, hydrate you, make you laugh until you snort… but I can't fix you. That's one reason why I call it Obstinate Spirituality. It ain't easy.

Sometimes healing deprives you of the lesson within illness. I call it the "healer's dilemma." Let's say you have a chronic pain and you come to me for a Reiki session to relieve that pain. I assist in that pain relief. End of story, right?

Nope.

What if that pain is a lesson that you chose to be born with in order to lead you to a higher purpose? If I take that away, then I have hindered your opportunity for personal growth. If I don't take the pain away, then I become an ineffective healer to you. Maybe as a result, you'd think that Reiki is a bunch of crap. Now, I've closed the door to any benefit you might derive from Reiki in other future circumstances.

Yes, nursing was a challenge given this awareness. Illness can be a teacher…sometimes the best. But I would have patients who were incapable of agreeing to have a Reiki treatment. So I would infuse their medications, their IV fluids, and their parenteral nutrition with Reiki. I would then ask their energetic body to choose what to do with the Reiki intention and to direct it to their highest and greatest good.

Maybe it went into the physical body. Maybe it went to a family member who was not ready for the patient's impending transition. Maybe it went back to the ether from which it came. Ultimately, I don't know, but I made it available.

Part of being a nurse is going to where the patient is at in that given moment. You make that connection and then try to bring them to where they need to be to facilitate healing. This is part of the art of nursing—that part they can't teach in school. You just have to learn by doing.

I had one patient who was an Old Testament scholar. After I administered his medications, I then spent time with him discussing the Dead Sea Scrolls, the Nag Hammadi, and how Peter essentially hijacked the religion away from Mary Magdalene and Jesus's brother, James. He said he'd never enjoyed being in a hospital so much.

You don't have to go the Gnostic Gospels! The accepted gospels mention that Jesus had four brothers: James, Joseph or Joses, Jude or Judas, and Simon. Several sisters are also alluded to in the same verses. Mary and Joseph rubbed sandals at some point. Repeatedly. James was older than Jesus, so how is Mary a virgin? Come on, man.

In a patrilineal society, virginity was just another state of ignorance that men used to confine women.

They used the Torah as a whip and not as a light.

No disrespect intended, but most people I've met who have a Bible and go around quoting it, have not bothered to question it. It is rife with inconsistencies.

Yes, 'I grew up Catholic and remained a Catholic until the age of reason', as George used to say.

Well, I can quote an excerpt from a cookbook, but it doesn't make me friggin' Bobby Flay. I'm saying that some holy rollers need to check themselves.

The fact of the matter is that Mary had two baby-daddies. And one skipped town and never paid child support.

Here's another napkin.

I know, I know. I'm probably gonna have to smoke a turd in Purgatory before I can get in. At least I know I'll be in good company.

What can I say? Trees don't grow straight up to Heaven and neither do I.

Cheers.

Guitars, Cigars and Tiki Bars

CHAPTER 12

Wounded Healers look at rules the same way a monster truck looks at curbs.

So, I have a question. You know how you can put your car in drive and the doors automatically lock? Good.

You know how cars have window tints of differing percentages but the film is comprised of a metal derivative? Good.

So my question is this: If we're so concerned about people killing other people while being distracted by their phones, why don't automakers turn the car into a Faraday cage when it's in drive, so that no signals can get in?

Every time you come to a stop light you can put your car in park, get a push from the phone service, and then go on with your day. If you need to talk, you can pull over.

Nah, a car's radio and navigation are hard-wired through the firewall.

I agree. We shouldn't legislate against stupidity, but we still do it. Seatbelt laws, child seat laws, bicycle and motorcycle laws...all smart decisions that had to have the gravitas of legal intervention.

Sometimes, you can't fix stupid. Sometimes, you can.

Maybe if we create a law where you can ride without a helmet after you do 10 hours of community service in a head trauma unit and agree to be an organ donor?

Dude, I get random thoughts like that all the time.

OK, here's another. Accordion cars.

Interlocking vehicle frame, like a cabinet drawer. You drive in compact mode throughout the week on solar power. When you want extra room to move stuff or to put the kayak on the roof, you release the connections, both physical and magnetic. The car then slides open like a drawer, *et voilà*! You now have an additional row like a minivan.

Why not? We've had amphibious cars, airplane cars, truck cars, so why not accordion cars? The El Camino may be the automotive equivalent of a 70's porn 'stache, but they have their place.

I don't know...ballistic-resistant materials interwoven with carbon fibers. Maybe electrical so that when charged it becomes rigid? I am not sure of the material science around it. I can just look at the world around me and apply what I see into different contexts.

What about you?

What inventions or creations do you have rolling around in your head? It's gotta be something good. Someone who could sit and listen to all that I have said without issuing a restraining order is someone pretty damned interesting.

Come on, gimme a good one.

Human augmentation without surgical intervention. Hmm...go on.

I know when we buy things there is an RFID chip either in them or on them. I know some clothing has RFID chips integrated into the label.

Yes, I have heard of people advocating for subcutaneous RFID. High-profile people have had those implants since the late 1980s. I know there was push back because it was seen as a way to track our movements So they put RFID in our clothes, credit cards, and passports. Between that and tracking our cell phones, we're tracked anyway.

Meh. Part of modern life. If you want to get away from it, all you need to do is go naked and leave your cell phone at home.

Cheers to Hedonism...One and Two!

Yeah, I remember heads-up displays, or HUDs, being discussed in the 90s. Started out in fighter jets and made it into high-end automobiles shortly thereafter. Nearly 30 years later and you don't see them in Ford Fiestas, now do you?

Huh! How about that? I didn't know they were collecting neural data while being used. Kinda like smart devices monitoring the room's conversations, I guess.

So, now we have algorithms that recognize our intent via neural conduction. Interesting. How would that interface work? Would you have to be wearing a hat of electrodes to convert that neural conduction to binary code?

Whoa! So the sensors are so delicately calibrated that they can pick up on our personal energetic field? I guess that would be akin to psychically connecting with your computer, but it's still technology interfacing in an unseen fashion. It's high tech Wi-Fi. But I see you're smiling...what are you holding back?

No way!

That's flipping awesome! You slowly dial back the sensitivity so that the human has to send stronger signals. It's training wheels for psychic communication.

Robert Bigalow said the next step in technology would be neural interaction with technology. Dude, the power of intention paired with the study of psionics is so underrated. That is a sweet idea!

So when are you going to create this?

It is? Where?

Elementary schools? Where?

What do you mean?

How can you know they're doing this in elementary schools sixty years from now? Are you from the future or do you project there?

Well, no wonder you have been sitting here and listening without calling the cops. I am so glad to meet another club member. How long have you been projecting?

Ha! Good answer. OK, this lifetime...how long have you been projecting?

That's amazing, dude. What is it about adolescence that starts the process of psychic abilities? I think there is more going on in the pituitary than western medicine says there is. After all, it looks like the Eye of Horus.

So tell me brother, what's your name?

Nice to meet you, Eugene.

OK, Hugh it is. So tell me, Hugh, you have been very accepting of my reality and you've admitted being able to astral project. What voodoo do you do?

No way! Soul fragment retrieval. I love it!

Here I am prattling away about my reality and you share a big chunk of that same reality. And you were such a good listener along the way! Most folks are quick to interrupt and reveal the commonality.

No. I just want to convey my gratitude for allowing me to get my message out of my head. It's been like a pressure cooker. Now that I have vented, I feel more serene inside. Again, thank you!

Dude, it drives me nearly insane. To have these experiences... to be compelled to share them... and to then be met with both ridicule and ambivalence? For more than a decade, I've been getting repeatedly knocked down. I do keep getting up, but I will admit is gets harder and harder every time... and I don't know how much more I can bounce. In fact, I don't bounce any more. I feel like I'm crapping a pot scrubber.

So, Hugh...blow my mind.

Seriously. There is fairness in reciprocity. I pushed your boundaries, I think, and it's only fair that you push mine. So, lay it on me.

Yes! I'm sure! Let it happen, captain.

OK.

Yes.

Yes, I have heard of that concept. Since souls are outside of time, and linear time is an illusion, then it is possible for a soul to inhabit two or more people who happen to be on Earth in the same time-space.

So, you are telling me you are aware of more than one concurrent meat suit?

Fascinating! How much do you recall of the other meat suit? Like, what's his name?

What can you tell me about Bob?

Black male. Single. Affinity for hot rods. You sound like my dad's friend, Bob, from Staten Island.

What? You are?!

No fucking way.

Really?

I need proof. Tell me more about Bob.

Yes.

Right.

Dude, this is pretty wild. But I have to admit that it all falls into my belief system.

No, it's not so much that I don't believe you. It's just surprising to have my beliefs validated…while drinking in a Tiki bar.

OK, my left brain is demanding answers.

What was Bob's name for his car and why?

Damn.

Yes, it was Miss Vicki and it was a 1951 Ford Victoria.

OK, maybe you did some deep research. That car was in several magazines back in the 1970s. I also think I mentioned it earlier. Give me something juicy.

Shit.

No. No one knew that.

No. There is no way he would have shared that with anyone. I mean...he grew up traveling around with a Green Book. In some towns in the South, you could be killed just for being black after sunset, so there is no way he would have shared that secret.

Still, I don't know. You may be a psychic or a channel and have picked up this information. Frankly, I don't know. But I am willing to go with it because I have missed my friend. His funeral—your funeral—was as terrible as it was beautiful to me.

What have I wanted to say? I want to say that I love you. I love you for being patient with me. I'm sure I annoyed you by asking you to speak "New York" for me.

It was so funny to my ear. Midwesterners have that flat accent that newscasts love. I'd never before heard a "New Yawker." I'd also never met a black man beyond saying hello to my dad's coworkers. I guess I should apologize, too, for all the times I wanted to touch your afro.

You were just so different from anything I knew. But the more time I spent with you, the more the differences faded. It was then that our similarities shone through. We loved cars, chrome, loud exhausts...

Yes! Cragar rims!

Yes! The wolf whistle horn you had hidden under the dash. God, I had so much fun with you and Dad riding around in that car! I still have an affinity for muscle cars today because of those times.

I'm so glad that you were in my life at such a young age! Just two years earlier, we were the only white family in the neighborhood and the kids picked on me something awful.

They stole my bike...they took my cowboy hat and my cap gun right out of my hands. They threw rocks at me for being white. Black kids scared me.

So that's why you were so tolerant. Did Dad ask you to do that?

Well, I'm glad you had the presence of mind to do it, anyway. You took the seeds of racism and you turned them into a plant that bore the fruit of tolerance. Damn, Bob, I can't tell you how thankful I am that we crossed paths. The world would have been a much scarier place. And I would have had such a limited view of the world. Your tolerance made me a better person. Wow...

Thanks. My turn with the tissues. OK, bar napkin.

Can we just sit here for a second?

Thanks.

Whew.

No, no need to apologize. This is good for me. I have been asking people to expand their way of thinking for decades. Now it's high time for me to have the opportunity to live my own words.

OK, I'm ready for more. Like Ali said, hit me again.

Yes, I am OK with you saying that you are both Bob and Hugh.

I'm sure. I am both a sea captain and me...and about a dozen other meat suits. So, I can wrap my head around you being both Bob and Hugh. Let's roll.

I think you came to me as Bob at a time in my life when events had started me down a path that could have been painful—possibly creating a limiting factor in my growth. I could have been a racist. And, through my connections as a musician and a nurse, I could have passed that negativity along to hundreds, maybe thousands, of others. If you had not intervened when you did, there's no telling...

Wait.

Shit...this is another intervention.

Holy shit balls! Are you an Ascended Master?

This sure as shit feels like an intervention...a visitation. Dude, there are no coincidences. You found me at a pivotal point in my childhood and here you are again.

No. I'm shutting up. Here I thought I was attempting to teach... to share with a member of John Q. Public... to elevate his thinking... to stimulate his dormant potential. Instead, I have been conversing with a master.

Please, there is a time and place for everything under Heaven. I thought it was a time to speak. This is a time to listen. I'm listening.

Huh? What do you mean I was auditioning?

OK.

Yes, I did say that a pivot can be challenging.

Yes, I did say that some people can pivot only so many times before they have had enough.

And that those people don't care how far they've come...that they are just so exhausted they'd rather go home than keep on fighting.

If you are who you claim to be then you know my answer.

Ah, free will. OK, yes, I know that pivoting can be painful, but after the pivot and the accommodation that follows, the new set of opportunities is priceless.

Well, back in 2009, I did not say I was agreeing to become a Reiki Master. I said that I was agreeing to be mastered by Reiki. So, I now say the same thing. The unknown potential that follows a pivot is worth the unknown pain.

I am agreeing to experience. I will participate in this variation of the Sun Dance.

I am listening, Hugh. What say you?

CHAPTER 13

YOLO? BS IMHO

John, my beloved brother, I want to congratulate you on your thirty-four lifetimes on this planet called Earth. Whilst you thus far have suspected you are on this Earth, and not of it, you should know your suspicion of extraterrestrial origin is correct. The first incarnation of your soul into the three-dimensional Universe was on a planet in the Mintaka star system—the rightmost star in Orion's Belt. One's first incarnation creates a template which fixes your predilections for all future 3-D incarnations. Your first incarnation fixed your path as Healer. You have self-identified as Healer-Warrior, Healer-Teacher, and Healer-Educator. You are a healer—first and foremost.

You have a strong sense of right and wrong and, as a consequence, you have lived and died for your beliefs over the course of many lifetimes. Where this would weaken the resolve of some, it distilled yours and has made your resolve more potent. This is reflected most notably in your Earthly incarnations as an American Indian medicine man in the 17th century, a Yamabushi Ronin in 16th-century Japan, a Vatican

Cardinal in the 14th century, and a Knight Hospitaller in the 12th century.

You entered this planet Earth knowing it was a master world. The duplicity and violence that this world potentiates is a reality not many souls can tolerate. To borrow from your nomenclature, for any soul to be on Earth is to be a "spiritual badass." You also selected one of the hardest human experiences to endure which you define as "abandonment."

It is a master assignment on a master world.

I, and the beings I represent, are honored to bear witness to your journey. We invite you to remember the energy wave forms of "admiration" and "reverence" we shared whilst you were visiting us with Source. Broadly speaking, these collective responses are not commonly bestowed and should be considered as such. You repeatedly choose the 'hero's journey', and oftentimes an external viewer would describe its culmination as "tragic."

You have done so very well in this current iteration with the life lessons herein: child abuse, bullying, heartbreak, betrayal, divorce, bankruptcy, coma, chronic illness, releasing your parents from life support, and your daily intractable pain. These hardships, or lessons, have resulted in younger souls returning home for restoration and reinsertion. And yet, you persisted. We honor your character, your tenacity, and approve of the nomenclature of your collective experiences as Obstinate Spirituality.

You have not only persisted, you have thrived. You have responded to your selected challenges in ways one would call heroic. You resisted death in your first days in an incubator. You saved your grandmother's life when you were in year six. You eased your grandfather's transition at nine. You saved your friend's life in year sixteen. You redirected others who were misguided in both the physical and spiritual realm through your astral projected interactions between your fifteenth and twentieth years. You assisted in the crossing over of scores of souls trapped in the location you visited called Dachau, Germany in your seventeenth year. You expedited the physical healing of several hundred others in your second and third decade with Reiki, music, and random acts of love. You saved your father from drowning in year thirty.

We saw that your choices were consistently leading you toward assisting, helping, and healing others while your concurrent life experiences should have made you bitter, angry, and blocked from Source. You freely elected to cross over misguided spiritual entities. You provided physical healing while you were homeless.

We inspired your classmates to provide you with appliances, home goods, kitchenware, and a bed. You are a good man doing good works; we assisted you by supplying for your needs. We intervened because you invited us to do so.

The White Brotherhood of the Medical Assistance Program began to work with you because of your tenacity. You have been, and continue to be, their instrument in both the physical and spiritual realm. We acknowledge your willingness to be an example of the "wounded healer" and have been marshaling the requisite forces to be ready for your summons.

May I continue?

Thank you.

Your music—voice, instruments, and composition—have been a conduit of healing for those who have lost hope. Your efforts redirected the consciousness of people to a time-space when things were better for them. Sometimes, a simple tune in their native language reached into a place where the ravages of dementia had not yet corrupted. This is why you have an affinity for Christmas carols. Recall that more than one person has told you that your song reminded them of prayer. Although you have performed before thousands at a time, it is your smallest performances which have resonated the farthest…and they echo up into Heaven itself just as the scent of honeysuckle arrests any present thoughts you have and elevates your consciousness. Remember this association.

We waited with anticipation when your voice appeared to be taken from you after your coma. We knew you had elected to have your voice taken away so that you could experience the feeling of having no voice in the literal sense so that you could embrace the nuance of not having a voice in the metaphorical sense. You inspired much curiosity from us when you elected to be compelled to convey a message and then to have your conduit for doing so taken from you. That challenge was observed by many in this realm. Your success was celebrated by even more.

Your "pre-corporeal" plan was approved by your master-guide because you wanted to explore the emotional context of the illusion of being ignorant of your inherent connection to Source beyond that which occurs to those who enter the physical incarnation on Earth. The price of admission to this reality is steep so creating a similar challenge willingly was most interesting because there was no guarantee that you would succeed. Free will *must* govern this physical reality. You chose not to be silenced and we celebrated your decision. You chose to cultivate another voice with your writing. We were pleased to see you made it so. This is why we greeted you with such enthusiasm whilst you were visiting. The irony is that you feel like you labor in obscurity. You feel like you are not seen. The opposite is true here.

With no other encouragement except a saying you wrote on your mirror—"For every mouth there are two ears"—you began writing short stories which were immediately published and distributed. From city, to state, to country, to the world, your written voice has traveled and flourished where your physical voice could not. We remind you of the thank-you notes you have received from around the world.

You have assisted those who have chosen the lessons of cancer, diabetes, heart disease, and arthritis through both the pharmaceutical research you performed and the clinical nursing you provided. You eased your patients through their lessons without judgment, and you offered solutions that may help them manage those lessons. Your efforts have been obscured from your human vision because your childhood abuse diminished your perceived value, and as a result, you believe your impact has been of little consequence. We reveal to you now that your collective efforts have assisted nearly nine million people around the world.

We are grateful for your twenty-year commitment to energy work and your deference as you allow us to work through you. We acknowledge your effort to prevent the dissonance of ego to diminish our work, but we also suggest you accept the emotion of pride in moderation. We have helped others dissipate their physical illnesses and emotional energy blocks masquerading as illnesses with your assistance. Through the process you identified as a 'shared near-death experience,' we have guided souls to the gates of Heaven. You do not speak of all your shared near-death experiences, but we are aware of your assistance and thank you for it.

You attempted to honor your father's admonishments in the course of your current time-space body even though you knew they were misguided. You were diminished by trying to honor him while in your third decade. That loss could not be permitted even within the framework of free will. So we initiated an intervention because you asked for help. We sent dreams, ancestral visitations, and life events to embolden you. Instead, you began the process you call your "soft suicide." You wrote in your journal after your bankruptcy and subsequent marital discord that you wished you could be in a coma and wake up when it was all over. We saw this as an invocation for assistance and we acted. You refer to this as your coma. More accurately, it was an intervention.

You were imbued with certain gifts upon your return. Some were immediate; some were downloaded but hidden as we still need to honor the rule of free will. You will remember them at a later date because your evolution has been accelerated. However, there is no guarantee that all of them will be revealed.

You agreed to be led back to your original path after a five-year period marked by divorce, NDE reentry turbulence, job loss, welfare, and the suicide of your mother. They were difficult—but necessary—lessons to get you back on your selected path and to prepare you for your personal evolution. Since then, two files have been revealed. Because more needs to be revealed, and because of your daily meditation, this current intervention is now possible.

We welcome you to ask aloud the question which you have formed in your mind.

You think you have fallen behind. You have not fallen behind. This implies the concepts of right and wrong. These concepts do not exist for us. You are learning; that learning rate ebbs and flows for all. Once again, the concept of irony is applicable. From our perspective, and to borrow from your vernacular, we refer to you as the Marathon Man because of your proclivity to sprint through iterations. Other souls are accustomed to having a corporeal experience, returning to their soul group, and then taking a period of respite to "chill out". When it was suggested that you stop incorporating into concurrent iterations from the energetic state, you agreed. You then began the process of accessing concurrent "meat suits" while in the corporeal state. Your choices are considered heroic, audacious, and irreverent. They are pleasing to many here. Still, your choices have once again made an intervention necessary.

I welcome you to verbalize another question.

You did come into this world to make certain specific contributions which will be challenging. While you were with us, you agreed to return, and you agreed to allow us to accelerate your growth so that these contributions could happen within the confines of this current time-space body.

You are correct that this is an intervention. You are again at a nexus of transition. But you need to hear certain affirmations which you have already encountered in a semiconscious state and in your dreams. We will state this in the physical Universe so that there is no equivocation.

You matter. You are loved unconditionally. You are a mentor to many in both the physical and spiritual realms.

Your contributions are not like those of a farmer. Farmers can see the evidence of their labors on a daily basis. Working with nature, they bring life into its fullest expression and can see that growth with every sunrise and sunset.

You are a fractal of nature. You facilitate environments for growth to occur, for things to flourish where they are, and as a result their chance for success is much greater. However, in that charge, you do not await the result. You do not see the benefit of your labors. After years of doing this work, you have become discouraged and have again questioned your worth.

Surrender that doubt.

You matter...more than you can know. This is because you have asked us specifically to withhold the full scope of your work and its effect until your return. This choice is another reason we continue to observe.

Yes, there are challenging times ahead. But within these challenges are lessons whereby all who have incarnated in this current time-space iteration have agreed to participate. The temptation to see these events as right and wrong will be great. As always—so long as you are human—you will have the freedom to choose how to perceive them and how they will serve you.

These challenging times will include atmospheric and planetary changes. They are the result of several extraterrestrial factors including increased solar activity, the area of three-dimensional space which the solar system is now moving through, the actions of terrestrial nonhumans, extraterrestrial humans, nonhuman Terran lifeforms, and non-Terran lifeforms.

In the near future, this area of space your galaxy is passing through will be referred to as The Briar Patch. However, the greatest of all these challenges are those stemming from humanity's own choices. Unfortunately, based on human behavior and genetic predilections, you must collectively experience conflict before you can collectively agree on harmony.

You may ask us another question.

Yes, you are correct in your hypothesis that this is part of the evolutionary process of the human experiment which is more than 100,000 years in the making and has required several iterations. Some smaller subgroups of early humans were able to achieve the necessary progress to participate in the ascension process. This was easier to achieve, as their population was smaller, their resources more abundant, and their development uninterrupted as they were in isolated groups. You would understand this early ascension experimentation as "proof of concept."

Yes, again, you are correct in your hypothesis. Human evolution is being simultaneously subjected to many variables, but you should be aware that the experiments have become increasingly complex over time. Several experiments are happening concurrently and their goals are diametrically opposed. A majority of these experiments are being done overtly while some are being done covertly. Both are being done by proxy for those beings who prefer to remain anonymous or who have been removed from the immediate solar vicinity. The concept of free will still exists, as well as the concept of choosing one's lessons prior to incorporating into a physical iteration, but the truthfulness of the choices is obscured.

You may ask us another question.

There are many paths by which humans may access their own innate wisdom, which is a part of Source. In point of fact, having access to Source is innately human. However, the power of that access is obfuscated by different instruments of control on this planet. Of all the paths available, one path is always within reach—pain. Pain is the one path that all humanity is familiar with and accustomed to experiencing. To avoid personal pain, one must cultivate other paths. To evolve beyond pain as a species, you must teach others to seek out other paths.

You may ask another question.

Yes, there are several extraterrestrial life forms present both within the solar system and on Earth. They have been here for more than 100,000 years. *Homo sapiens*, as a species, are the result of multiple hybridizations and iterations. These extraterrestrials are well aware that the soul can incarnate into different physical iterations and they have spent millions of years creating multiple bipedal variations.

Each variation has different proclivities. What is unique about this most recent iteration of humans is the breadth of emotional response that they are capable of demonstrating. What is uniform about the human experiment is that every iteration works toward ascendance and that their reach extends beyond their grasp.

You have associated your path with that of the Jungian archetype of the wounded healer. And so it is. Chiron, the half-brother of Zeus, has been your model because of his extraordinary healing abilities and because centaurs demonstrate the healing properties associated with exploring the pleasures of the five senses. To borrow one of your sayings, 'Do it 'til it hurts…3 to 4 times to be sure.'

Yes, this suits your current set of proclivities.

Although Chiron sustained a wound that was considered fatal, he was a Titan; he could not die. The result of this paradox was that Chiron would spend eternity in excruciating pain. It is because of this pain that Chiron achieved transcendence and became known as a legendary healer. Plato reinforced this notion. According to him, the most skillful physicians "are those who have suffered from all sorts of illnesses." It is essentially the fundamental principle of both human spiritual evolution and modern medicine. And, like many things of this Earth, it is also an illusion.

You have said this to yourself many times, but I ask you now to stop, and know this: Your karmic debt is paid in full.

In fact, there never was a debt. There is no sin for which you need to atone. There is no judgment from Source, as Source is unconditional love. In truth, there are only lessons and love.

You are welcome to relive any pain you desire as this is the nature of free will. But know that it is not necessary.

You have never been bound to any construct except in your mind. Therefore, I speak to your mind and I tell you, you are released from that cycle from this day forward.

Know that when you choose to lay this burden aside, you will be ready for the next evolution as well as the magic and mystery it brings.

I must now ask for your forgiveness. You have accurately deduced that I am from a future in this Earth reality. You have also deduced that I am the soul of the person you and your father knew as Bob. There is one more iteration that you need to know, and rather than present it to you in concrete form, I have made a play on words to see if I could have you guess it. I told you I am called Eugene or Hugh. This is a play on the homophonous relationship of "Hugh" and "You." Just as you have learned to project back to previous lifetimes to engage in the process of soul fragment retrieval, your next physical iteration is interested in more than fragments. Your next iteration returns to previous lifetimes as another might return to a favorite movie or book.

Yes, John. I am the next corporeal version of you. Please continue to refer to me as Hugh so there is less cognitive dissonance.

There is no change in my duty to you in this moment of intervention. My message to you is undiminished. You are ready to pivot. We are there for you. Remember the angel's song. You belong to us.

You have asked and it is so given. We now await your decision on what you will do with your gift.

Now, what say you, John?

Guitars, Cigars and Tiki Bars

CHAPTER 14

Dating: Reality   *Relationship status:* Complicated AF

"Well…shit the bed."

"Indeed," replied Hugh.

"I'm at a loss for words. And that is saying something for me."

"Trust me, I know," said Hugh through a broadening grin.

"So, isn't some space-time continuum being broken here?"

"You tell me. You tell you."

"Well, I would speculate that since consciousness is energy and energy is connected to everything, then us occupying the same point in time and space is moot."

"We are in agreement. Continue."

"So we can sidestep the potential psychic harm of discussing our future selves and their actions. However, the time traveler's paradox is still in play because if you were to kill me, it would fundamentally change who you are. It would change the toolbox you used in your lifetime to become who you are, right?"

Hugh replied, "Theoretically, yes. Imagine your life as a train track where the first car of the train is a machine that lays the track. Behind you is a solid, immovable track. Before you is no track at all. But as soon as you have charted a direction, the track is laid and the engine is already upon the rail."

"Think of life as not a singular experience, but rather as a series of possibilities with different degrees of potentiality. Moment to moment, you are manifesting your reality with the choices you make. You are unequivocally co-creating with the Universe. The delay from thought to action is where the Universe receives your intention, commits to that particular possibility, recalculates the new set of possibilities, and then reshapes the physical Universe around you and the other co-creators in your life."

"Well, Hollywood and game developers have certainly made some serious jack from the premise —what happens when a given individual chooses the path not traveled. But I still don't have an answer to the question. Are you here to whack me to change your toolbox?"

"No, my brother, there is no ill will here. While your life is yours to live and your free will is not affected, once you have committed to a course of action, then it is set. That being said, as with any rule, it can be broken. However, there are consequences for rule breaking. The Universe is a system of systems and each system has a course correction feature. Not only is the course corrected, but the error within the system is also corrected."

"Whoa—so if I were to change the past, not only will the Universe put things back the way they were, but it would also stop me from doing it?"

"The Universe would attempt to correct all of the affected variables so that this timeline would still meet its unique objectives. This set of tracks—one of many millions—accomplishes a particular set of goals. Adjustments are made to ensure those goals are met."

"And me?"

"There would be an intervention similar to a situation in which a programmer discovers a bug in the software."

"Well, that sure as shit sounds ominous. What about free will? If I choose to go back and create havoc, then…"

"Your thoughts become things in alternate Universes. A new train is created and a new track is begun. And it is not as ominous as you think. We will borrow your metaphor from earlier—if you were a second-grade student reading James Joyce, and were fully capable of understanding the literary theory behind it, then you would be observed, tested, and monitored. Your existence would not be halted."

"So, I am hearing that free will exists in theory only. I can choose to make a series of decisions that will eventually cause the system to intervene."

"You are correct. There are systems of controls in place to provide course corrections. Race, gender, nationality, religion, politics, education, familial expectations—for most people, all these moving parts buffer people's choices. But occasionally, there are people like you who have challenged the system. You have chosen to opt out of many of these systems. As a nonconformist, you were monitored and evaluated on several occasions and by several groups. It was decided to invite you into our group."

"We introduced you to our group at a supraconscious level, explained the goals we hoped to achieve, and asked if you would like to participate with us. While you agreed to participate in our quest, you also were limited in your exposure. You asked to be allowed to continue on the track unaffected until the time for intervention arrived. That time has arrived."

"And now it has arrived?"

"And now it has arrived."

"So what now, Eugene, the dance machine?"

"The intervention you and I are having now is different from what we originally intended. Your energetic explorations have worn thin the barriers between the supraconscious, the subconscious, and the conscious realities; they are now semipermeable. Because you have begun piecing it together in your conscious state, we have made adjustments accordingly."

"Your assessment of being a 'spiritual paramedic' is accurate. While every human on the planet has the capacity to do what you have done, not many have actually done it. Collectively, the whole human race is discovering that the aforementioned religious, financial, familial, and ecological support systems are disguised systems of control. As they are waking up, they are reaching out to find other systems of control. This is both understandable and blunted effort. A more precise response is for people to reach within. This is what you have done, and you have done it in several ways. If you choose to do so, you can offer mentorship to those who choose to listen. In turn, we will mentor you."

"Great. I'm a metaphysical guinea pig...the nail that stands the tallest."

"If that is what you choose, then it will be so. That is the nature of this reality. But I offer you another possibility. You were a teacher-mentor as evidenced by your occupation as an English teacher. You were a teacher-mentor as evidenced by your occupation as a nurse. You were a teacher-mentor as a technical trainer. You were a teacher-mentor to a child that the educational system had abandoned. You are a teacher-mentor who speaks from both what they have learned and from what they have experienced. You synthesize traditional learning and experiential learning styles into a banquet table from which all may find sustenance."

"There are so many methods for negotiating the societal pitfalls that exist in the system, and within one physical being—you—several exist: meditation, astral projection, ancestral communication, past life regression, energetic healing, near-death experiences, and pharmacodynamics. Any one of these can be life altering for a human being. Any one of them could also be the limit of a human being's curiosity or their capacity to bear. You carry several. This is why you were surrounded with admiration when you were with us. This is why there was an intervention. This is why there is a new agreement or "course correction." Your soul's first incarnation set the mold. Thousands of years ago, your soul was conceived to serve, educate, elevate, and protect."

"Wow. I wish my friggin' high school counselor could hear this. It would melt his noodle."

"An apt expression considering the circumstances. And, if I may add, more acceptable than defecating where one sleeps."

"Dude, no offense, but I'm exhausted just hearing about this. I get tired just thinking about going back out there and trying to tell my story. I have been rejected so many times. It just feels like an exercise in futility. It feels like rolling a rock up a big damn hill...forever."

"It is what you decide it is...from moment to moment."

"I just need to let this steep a bit."

"While you are contemplating this conundrum, let me ask you other questions. Why did you choose to call your spirituality 'Obstinate Spirituality'?"

"Grandma said I was as stubborn as a mule with a nail in its head. Sometimes, when life events became greater than my capacity to understand, the only thing that kept me going was my stubbornness."

"Would you agree that a person's stubbornness would be interpreted by another as tenacity?"

"Sure."

"Would you say the source of one's tenacity is experience?"

"Sure. You learn to tough it out because somewhere earlier you learned that you can weather the storm."

"From that mental space of 'weathering the storm', while the tempests blow and the sky cries above, you have several emotions being expressed concurrently. Fear and resolve are the loudest. But what would you say is the strongest? What would you say is the root or the wellspring of those emotions?"

"Hope."

"Hope is one of the most prized human emotions we witness from our vantage point. Marshaling your forces on an idea when you are unsure of the outcome is a concept we are unfamiliar with on the other side. It is an amazing and inspirational process to witness."

"But there are times when you are in situations that you have no frame of reference. You do not have the benefit of experiential learning. From that perspective, what do you draw upon?"

"Knowledge, I guess...I mean, you consider all the variables before you, and then you choose the path that you think will give you the best outcome. But knowledge is only part of the equation because humans don't make decisions based on facts alone. Our emotions, perceptions, and experiences shape the knowledge—both the internalization and expression of it."

"Very good. So, I will parse it differently and ask the question again. When you are at a crossroads and both paths appear identical but they curve off in different directions so that your extended view is blocked, what do you do? What well do you draw from for inspiration?"

"Ha! You're leading me. And 'inspiration' is a big clue. But, you're right. It's faith. In the absence of hope, one needs faith. Even when it is dark outside, I know the sun still shines. But I'll tell you, there were times in my life I don't think I had emotional access to either hope or faith. Whatever it was, it did not feel like faith or hope."

"Interesting. What did it feel like?"

"Inertia."

"And where did that trajectory carry you? Did it weigh you down or did it buoy you up?"

"Well, if it had weighed me down, I would not be wearing this meat suit right now. But there were times when I don't think it lifted me up either. It just got me through the situation. Kind of like running naked through a corn field. You get through, but you sustain a thousand cuts along the way."

"And do you think the next time you find yourself in such a situation you might be inspired to invoke some protection?"

"Hell, yes! I'll do more than wear protection. I'll wear an inflatable sumo suit!"

"And *this* is why people will listen. You carry much knowledge but you carry yourself as though you don't. A person's voice is a sum of their experiences. Since your experiences are unique, so, too, is your voice. People will listen. In fact, there are some people who will resonate with your energy specifically and will need to hear what you say."

"That sounds pretty unlikely, Hugh. I usually have to wear a red polo and khakis at a Target just to get people to talk to me."

"That is about to change. At this moment in time, people need hope, faith, and laughter. They will seek it as roots seek out water. In some ways, it will be subtle and beyond your vision. In other ways, it will be as obvious as a root breaking stone."

"And with that being said, my time here has come to a close. Know that there are legions cheering you on and dozens along your path awaiting the opportunity to assist you with your mission. We cannot make choices for you, but we can facilitate a smoother pathway once you have made them. In your selection criteria, we would ask you to also choose to be kind to yourself."

"Thanks, dude. I guess the first thing I need to say is thank you for your help. If each 'iteration'—which sounds a lot better than 'meat suit'—is growing in complexity and relationships, then I *really* need to thank you! I guess I've been keeping you busy."

"Yes, you have. But it has been a pleasing experience," said Hugh.

"And based on my reception party during my NDE, I thought I was providing entertainment for those who weren't ready to put their toe in the water. There was such adoration and respect—it felt foreign and familiar at the same time. It was a lot to take in. It still is."

"Agreed. But, you have. And we here are deeply honored to have been witness," said Hugh.

"But, homie, I also need to thank you for the affirmation. I had bits and pieces of this in my head, but I was not sure what was real, what was a dream, and what was the result of too many Old Fashions. I need to work on my discernment. Most of what you said is something that has been revealed to me. I have heard it just as I was waking up. I have had larger chunks of it imparted to me in a dream state shortly before waking up. Snippets of information have even come to me in between hitting the snooze button."

Hugh replied, "Yes. Again, the energy separating your different layers of consciousness have become more harmonized over time. This is part of the ascension process we hope to see for all mankind."

"But it's a hot mess. Dude! Some of the information is actionable. Some of it is foreshadowing. But I'm not sure how much of it is verbatim and how much of it is symbolism that requires a bit of interpretation. I mean…come on…my dream journal is full of single words or a sentence or two."

Hugh smiled.

"And more recently, I will be going along with my day, and then I will have an episode of déjà vu. Except it is not something I have seen or done beforehand. It will instead trigger a memory of a dream. And what the hell do you call that anyway? Just like when I dream a variation of my OBEs…what do you call a dream about a memory of something that never happened in this physical reality? I guess I'd call it precognition stuck in granny gear."

Hugh nodded for me to continue.

"I guess if I really want to know, I can spelunk that rabbit hole and figure it out. I've heard that for a couple of years now from different people. It's funny. I go in for a reading and the psychic tells me I should be doing a reading for them. Again, I know part of it is discernment. But I also don't feel compelled to be a card table soothsayer. It's too confining."

"Now, don't get me wrong. I appreciate the talent. I mean, if it were carpentry, I know immediately that I'd like it. But I also know that I would be looking for a greater challenge down the road."

"It's a great tool for the tool belt, but there is more to do. I've seen it in my hypnagogic state, and I have seen it repeatedly. I'm on stage with a heavy, oxblood colored curtain behind me and a follow spot obscuring any view of the audience. I feel that I am talking to a few hundred people. As I'm talking, I am also thinking this is why I was a musician. I can be on stage and I'm not intimidated by it. In a way, it's comforting."

Hugh sipped his drink but continued to listen.

"I also see interviews: podcasts, radio, TV. The awareness of speaking, traveling, teaching, learning, sharing...it is both empowering and humbling at the same time. So, too, nursing and pharmaceutical training. It's just another part of my life that was also preparation."

"The thing that scares me most is not the pivot, but the amount of fuel I have left in the tank. If this pivot gets sideways on me, will I have the muscle to bring it around? Will I have the fortitude to hang on until I can get my bearings? Seriously, I am at a stage in life where I should be hyper conservative, putting all my pennies away for retirement, and remaining under the radar until then."

"Seriously?" asked Hugh.

"You're right...even as the words came out of my mouth, I knew I would not take that path. I am what I am because of the choices I have made. I also have made the choices I have made because of who I am."

Hugh sat silently, but his eyes twinkled with expectation.

"Alright, damn it, I choose the pivot. Because of who I am, but—more importantly—because of who this means I can potentially become. I can assist others as well as myself. They can teach me so I may teach others. I can add even more amazing things to my metaphysical toolbox to assist others while in this iteration and the ones that follow."

Hugh revealed a broad, gracious smile. "Thank you, John, for agreeing to this. By doing so, we are now allowed to set in motion several things we have queued up in anticipation. You are about to receive a phone call from a book publisher. Take the call and follow that path. We will be ahead of you making sure the path is clear. Remember that you have earned this. You have paid a very high price, but you deserve all the good things which are to come. Yes, there will be challenges. But there will also be rewards which you have not yet dreamt. Remember, you are loved more than you know…and by people whom you have never met.

"And one last thing—'Me, too'."

Guitars, Cigars and Tiki Bars

EPILOGUE

Dear Humanity — Please start behaving like there's a "Come to Jesus" spanking looking for an ass to happen.

I hear you.

I hear you because there was a time not so long ago that it was my own voice saying it—this dude is full of bullshit. While the literary framework around my premise is complete fiction, my story is true. Granted, I'd like to hang out at Tiki bars with a cold, fruity adult beverage and have some awesome discussions with friends I have yet to meet, but it has not yet come to my reality.

There are so many times I tried to tell my story. If you have read to this point, I thank you for being one of the few who, like my childhood friend, Bob, are making the time to listen. The time wasn't right then, but I have been told it is now.

I hope you found it was at least entertaining and maybe even educational. To be a positive influence in a person's life, even someone I may never meet, is one of the joys I have while being alive.

I've heard it said that the Kingdom of Heaven lies within. So, too, salvation. Still, I fell into the trap of seeking resolution in a church. Camaraderie, education, music, advice—these are what you find in a church. I made the mistake of going to a building to find that balm they sing of in church hymns. To reinforce my error, the minister gave me *that* look. You damn sure don't need to be psychic to look into someone's eyes as they lose interest. There have been other times when I can hear the old-fashioned, spring-loaded screen door of their asses slamming shut.

Given all my travels—physical universe and otherwise—I still make mistakes. I was not thinking clearly in that moment. I was piecing my life back together after divorce when my mom's suicide demanded what was left of my sanity. I was in a dark place...maybe the darkest I've ever been. And that's saying something when you consider a demonic spirit had tried to hijack my body.

But Obstinate Spirituality kept me going. In the near future, I believe we all can benefit from cultivating our own version of Obstinate Spirituality. More than winter is coming.

Even as I write these words, I am not certain what my ultimate intention is for this literary effort. But I can tell you with complete sincerity that I believe I needed to get this out of my head and into the world for someone's benefit. My OS has helped me in dark places. Maybe it will help others.

It is here Ovid speaks the loudest to me. Look up a quote of his that speaks to you and pretend I wrote it. My vibe here is that mankind and his selfish behaviors have run up a karmic debt that is going to get called. The 1%'rs are going to stick us with the bill and we'll be left having to set things right.

If you are not practiced in the art of surrender, there is a spark that follows soon thereafter. It is the potential of thought about to form into physical reality. As above, so below. This spark, for me, becomes words that fall onto a page. With these words, a movie also plays in my head. Watch it with me.

Fade in on an aging but determined pitcher whose best seasons are behind him. He is one pitch away from winning a hard-fought game. As the rain beads up on his weathered face and calloused hands, he looks at the ball as though he is seeing it for the first time.

This child's toy is a reflection of his life. Toughened hide, stitches, scars, scratches—that which was pure and clean at the start is no more and never will be again. However, this game is not yet done. Does he throw down or does he throw away? A long-neglected ember of the mind bursts forth into flame. Upon his face, an unfamiliar smile blooms and a decision is made. He digs in.

Here's my wind up.

One person's reality may not match your own, but it can sure as hell shape your behavior. There is a saying that a sweater is something you put on when your mom is cold. You may decide to put on a sweater to humor her or you may decide not to and risk the glare of derision that will probably follow. Neither choice is right or wrong.

It does not necessarily follow that your garment selection reflects your love or connection with her. She is still your mom. She has cleaned both of your sloppy, stinky ends and was loving enough to use a different washcloth for each...as far as you know.

While all of this book's aforementioned explorations into human potential are true for me, they may not be true for you—at least for right now. And that's OK because I am not asking you to buy what I'm selling; I'm not asking you to buy the sweater.

I'm asking you to look at it, see if it is something you want to consider trying on, and then you can decide to wear it. Or you can destroy it in a ceremony of your choosing and hit the holy water hot tub. Free will, brothers and sisters.

But before you grab thy holy hand grenade and chuck it at me, having reached the counting of three, let's first review the things you and I have in common because the things that bind us are the important things.

We are:

- Hairy in all the usual places
- Eating things we probably shouldn't
- Drinking things we probably shouldn't
- Loving our family despite their flaws
- Working on loving our self despite our flaws
- Cussing while on the highway
- Missing terribly the loved one's we've lost
- Crying when we're heartbroken
- Planning how to spend our lottery winnings
- Watching more porn than we should
- Watching less of nature than we should
- Regretting a lost love from our past
- Celebrating that rash that went away
- Regretting sneezing while on medicinal laxatives
- Wondering if we'll ever be out of debt

You and I are so much alike. Still, we are not harvested from petri dishes so there will be variations. Thank God... Goddess...

or whatever proper noun floats your ark. The world needs to be filled with more than just white Ford Fiestas.

Color, gender, height, physical proportions, number of teeth, sexual orientation, a smattering of freckles...these things are differences so that we can recognize each other in a crowd. They do not change any of our true commonalities.

There are regional differences too: accents, dialects, food choices, religious influences, clothing selections, outdoor activities. Still, they are nothing more than variations of a truth.

The truth is, the things that make us human, are not the things on the outside. What makes us human are the things on the inside. I learned this in college, but I came to understand it on the oncology floor of the hospital in which I worked.

Cancer survivors will tell you they don't really sleep. The nausea, pain, and worry are always there. Occasionally, they get an opioid push resulting in their consciousness being turned off, but they are not really resting. So when I worked the midnight shift, I had time to visit with my patients as they recalled the day's events or contemplated their future.

My patients wore hospital gowns. They were not wearing the latest styles nor the brightest jewelry. Their status symbols, from hair(style) to hubris, were gone. Their autonomy was stripped from them as they were bathed, fed, dressed, and wiped. With all the illusions gone, before me was still a human being. Sometimes, they needed to be reminded of that and it was an honor to be that person.

You, dear reader, and I are human beings. From this sacred space, I will tell you of my human experience and its associated realities with both clarity and brevity.

Ghosts are real. If you want to believe me, I challenge you to go to a hospital where a wing is closed, dress up in scrubs, sit in a hallway and wait. Same thing with schools, battlefields, baseball stadiums, and churches. Expect to hear unexplained sounds, smell unexplained smells, or feel something.

Spiritual Death is not real. You can go back, reincarnate, and finish your list of lessons either with the same people or with another set of people providing you the opportunity to finish the list. It's your choice.

No matter how brilliant they are, doctors are human and don't know everything. They will need to be "re-reminded" of spontaneous recoveries, the placebo effect, and bodies we possess other than physical.

Reiki reorganizes one's life in a positive way. If it doesn't serve you, it will be removed. If you choose to become a Reiki Master, you are agreeing to be mastered by Reiki. Let go or be dragged.

You are already having out-of-body experiences. You identify them as weird dreams, *déjà vu*, or daydreams.

Consciousness is not a single door but a ladder. The rungs are daydreaming, remote viewing, astral projection, dreams, and sleep. On each rung, work can be done.

Time is an agreed upon construct prior to incarnation. It is tied to gravity and both can be manipulated.

Distance is subjective. In Newtonian physics, distance equals time multiplied by velocity. How do you measure distance when I can be in my home in the U.S. and then be standing next to the London Eye... in 2009... a few minutes later?

Sorry to piss on your Pop-Tarts™, but there are aliens among us. In fact, some have been here before humans were even contrived. My projection intention was this—show me something interesting on the moon. After a few deep breaths, I found myself in a hanger bay that reminded me of the scene of the rebel base on Hoth in the Star Wars movies. Frankly, I was disappointed. I was expecting a DeLorean and I found a

Rambler. The place was dirty, dusty, poorly lit and the ships I saw were our equivalent of busted up hoopdies.

Coming out from behind the craft I had just examined was a reptilian being who stood a bit over 7 foot tall. He was bored, startled, curious, and threatened all at the same time. Based on the mental exchange and chase that followed, I'm sure they would prefer their presence remain obfuscated.

The bill for the generations of negligence we have perpetrated on the planet has come due. We're all going to go through some collective growing pains. It's time to get our heads and asses wired together.

Humanity's training wheels have come off. We need to stop others from being an ass to the planet and her creations!

If you have been distracted or are just waking up, let's review.

Our solar system is hitting speed bumps. Sometimes referred to as the heartbeat of Earth, the Schumann Frequency has a measurable resonance of about 7.8 MHz. We have been spinning through space in areas where the frequency was over 90 MHz. Think people are irritated when the refrigerator or the overhead lights hum? This dissonance can make people as irritable as a cheese grater scrubbing their pink parts.

The Earth's magnetic poles are moving. There are areas where gravity is not consistent. Weather changes are getting worse. Fukushima has been dumping radioactive water into the ocean long enough for cesium to show up in Alaskan salmon and Vancouver goat cheese. There are now three gyres or islands of trash nearly twice the size of Texas between China and California. Pollinators are dying off. Crop biomass is shrinking. Corporations are locking down clean water sources.

Look around you! All of our systems are becoming disrupted: religion, finance, technology, sexuality, politics. Things are no longer working when we impose a simplistic yes/no answer to very complex systems.

Consider running this idea past your stereotypical Fox News demographic—your new neighbor can have a child born of three parents, raised in an atheistic household, and lovingly run by homosexual spouses. Imagine this child will be home schooled while living in a cooperative. They become an entrepreneur, finance their company through crowd funding, and use the ethical influence the company wields as a B-Corp to elevate a triple bottom line. Your other young neighbors will enter into a mufti-generational, poly-amorous relationship and propagate in vitro children of their own in order to decide which genes to activate before the zygote is in utero.

I posed a variation of this question to my septuagenarian neighbor and the first question I got was telling.

"Are they or their children going to be baptized?"

The next question was interesting, too. "How are they going to get a mortgage without a credit score?"

The point is our support systems, which are not keeping pace with change, are losing support and will eventually implode—usually taking along innocent victims.

And those who are trying to cling onto those vestiges of a dying paradigm are dying—and they, too, are sometimes taking innocent victims along with them. Just as last century's lamplighters and wheelers are no longer needed, so, too, this generation's cashiers, delivery drivers, bartenders, and fast food workers.

Humanity is going to have so many stressors that we will be forced to be nice to each other or we're going to die in the process.

To be clear, we're all going to get scraped and bruised over the next few decades. Being able to tap into some metaphysical aspect of your humanity will preserve your sanity and give you the strength to keep calm(er) and carry on. Once we're through The Briar Patch, we will have a renaissance like humanity has never known before. While the children who will see this conversion are not yet born, we can dig the wells now from which they will drink. In the spirit of clarity, we are also going to either be part of, or be witness to, some of the most horrific things humanity has ever seen. Again, back to the OS.

Humanity has been an experiment that has been going on for tens of thousands of years. Ice ages, meteors, and floods have occasionally wiped the slate clean as upgraded iterations were introduced. But like all experiments, the time has come to prep the results, present the findings, and see what outcomes follow.

Why now? The Mayans had it correct. The old cycle ended in 2012 and a new cycle began. Our society did not fall, but the sociological structures that hold up our society reached the end of their service life.

Why you? If you have read this far, then you are part of the crew that is responsible for trying to bring people back from the extremes and point them towards the future. It is the end of an era but not the end of life.

Why now? According to a Pew Research survey around 2007, about 10 Million Americans a year have a near-death experience. Nearly all of those people come back with a download of new information which includes a call...no, an obsession, to help their fellow man in whatever way they can. If necessary, they will abandon their family, their job, their home, and their religion to carry out their mission. If it's 10 Million Americans a year, then how many people currently have this compulsion globally? How many total in the decade that followed this report?

Some people do not report their NDE, so this number is low. There is also a subset of people who have the NDE experience and fallout without the pesky "death" aspect. These are the people who achieve satori through all the other metaphysical on-ramps we discussed. How many people in the world have achieved this through prayer, meditation, fasting, exercise, drugs, or other epiphanies?

When I was trying to assess my mental stability after my own NDE, I was able to volunteer my services as a medical research professional and read through hundreds of tests, questionnaires, and diaries to piece together a typical patient profile for these NDE people. A template evolved from my research and they clinically looked like another fragmented subset of society—alien abductees.

Whether real or imagined, their clinical presentation was nearly identical to those with PTSD following an abduction. Both groups got a download, both could not tolerate the lifestyle they returned to, and both had a compulsion to make the world a better place while risking their own personal survival.

For argument sake, if 20 Million people a year were being "tuned up" worldwide over the past decade, there should be 200 Million people out there with a download designed to bring the world into a state of preparation—if not illumination. There should be a chorus of voices who are much stronger than mine shouting from the rooftops to whispering in the alleys. And if you are reading this, I think you are part of the chorus.

In some places, people refer to the second coming of Christ being dispersed in a Pentecostal fire rather than be imbued within one person. The second coming might be all of the EHE folks having a file folder that opens for us simultaneously. Rather than one messiah, we'll have millions of mini-me messiahs around the world.

This book, if it does nothing else, is my equivalent of shouting, 'come out, come out, wherever you are.' It's getting late, people. The training wheels have come off. I implore you to get off the bench and get in the game before it gets called because of bad weather.

I'll see you on the field.

ABOUT THE AUTHOR

John is a graduate of Marian University in Indianapolis and holds degrees in Music Performance (Voice), English Literature (Secondary Education) and Nursing (Oncology and Informatics). He is a Clinical Research Nurse who has worked in pharmaceutical research since 1996.

His ADD has rewarded him with several hobbies including selling an organic skin cream infused with Reiki and home-made tinctures, furniture restoration and retasking, motorcycle riding, and writing. He was in the vanguard of internet based clinical trials and is a platform member of IBM-Watson Health.

John has used his teaching skills to create classes meeting FDA regulations and to train WHO clinicians, opinion leaders, and researchers from around the world. He used these skills to create his own classes.

His classes range from using applied metaphysics to increase patient reported outcomes in healthcare settings to teaching people how to do remote viewing and astral projection.

He also does public speaking engagements covering his personal experiences of spirit communication, Reiki, remote viewing, past life regression, astral projection. Most recently, while under medical supervision, he experienced episodes of trans-dimensional awareness and met The Architect. Additional talks, classes, and literature will be forthcoming.

John is divorced and lives in Durham, NC with his black cat and Labrotty dog. His primary website is www.johnmathis.me. His Facebook page is www.facebook.com/GCandTB.

Guitars, Cigars and Tiki Bars